Green **Line**

3

von
Elizabeth Daymond
Elise Köhler-Davidson
Anja Treinies

herausgegeben von
Harald Weisshaar

Ernst Klett Verlag
Stuttgart · Leipzig

Hallo liebe Schülerinnen und Schüler,

mit Green Line 3 Vokabeltraining aktiv kannst du die neuen Vokabeln aus deinem Englischbuch üben.

Es ist immer gut, neue Wörter in einem Satz zu lernen. Du findest daher zu jeder Seite in deinem Schulbuch unter „What do you remember?“ englische Sätze, die du am besten mit Bleistift vervollständigen kannst. Dabei helfen dir auf der linken Seite deutsche Sätze mit den dick gedruckten Lernwörtern aus deinem Buch, deren englische Entsprechungen du rechts in die Lücken der englischen Sätze eintragen sollst. Manchmal gibt es aber auch statt der Sätze Bilder als Hinweis darauf, was in die Lücke gehört.

Hier zwei Beispiele:

Das Wetter sei **enttäuschend** gewesen und der Regen habe erst **zwei Tage zuvor** aufgehört.	The weather had been ____________ and the rain had only stopped ____________ .	☐
	But he said that his host family had given him a warm ____________ and they had been very friendly.	☐

Deine Lösungen kannst du auf den Seiten 70–79 selbst überprüfen. Achte dabei auch auf die korrekte Schreibung der Wörter. Hast du dich an die richtigen Wörter erinnert und sie fehlerfrei geschrieben, kannst du in die Kästchen am Rand ein Häkchen setzen.

Notiere die Wörter, bei denen du Schwierigkeiten hattest, und lerne sie noch einmal. Du kannst z. B. Karteikarten mit den Wörtern anlegen und damit üben. Versuche dann erneut, die Sätze zu vervollständigen.

Wenn du alle Kästchen abhaken kannst, beherrschst du alle wichtigen Wörter dieser Seite, du hast also deine Vokabeln gut gelernt. Du kannst außerdem versuchen, die englischen Übungssätze links zuzuhalten und die deutschen selbst zu übersetzen. So kannst du alles noch einmal wiederholen und festigen.

Zusätzlich gibt es noch viele Rätsel und andere spannende Aufgaben für dich, damit du die neuen Wörter üben und ausprobieren kannst. Diese findest du immer unten auf jeder Seite.

Viel Spaß und Erfolg mit deinem Vokabeltraining aktiv!

Inhaltsverzeichnis

Unit 1 The world of sport

→ pages 8/9

What do you remember?		
Um **Baseball** zu spielen, braucht man einen  .	In order to play ______ you need a ______ .	☐
Es ist ein beliebter **amerikanischer** Sport.	It is a popular ______ sport.	☐
Man spielt es auf einem **Spielfeld**.	You play it on a ______ .	☐
Die Spieler schlagen einen Ball und rennen von **Base** zu **Base**.	The players hit a ball and run from ______ to ______ .	☐
Ein/e **Schiedsrichter/in kontrolliert** ein Fußballspiel.	A ______ ______ a football match.	☐
Das **Spielfeld** ist 90 bis 120 Meter lang.	The ______ is 90 to 120 metres long.	☐
Man spielt **Rugby** mit einem **ovalen** Ball.	You play ______ with an ______ ball.	☐
Trage immer einen **Helm**, wenn du **Skateboardfahren** gehst.	Always wear a ______ when you go ______ .	☐
Wenn man **Leichtathletik** macht, rennt man oft auf einer **Laufbahn**.	If you do ______, you often run on a ______ .	☐

1 Sports

Fill in the missing words to complete the descriptions of the following sports.

referee track controls run American pitch bat base throw base hits hands

1 
You play it on a ______ . Usually, you mustn't use your ______ . A ______ ______ the match.

2 
There is a 400-metre ______ where people ______ . They also ______ balls or jump.

3 
It is a popular ______ sport. A player ______ the ball with a ______ and then runs from ______ to ______ .

→ pages 8/9

What do you remember?

Um Tennis zu spielen braucht man einen  .	In order to play tennis you need a ______ .
Der **Schiedsrichter** sieht den ganzen **Tennisplatz.**	The ______ sees the whole tennis ______ .
Ein **Kricket**spiel kann 5 Tage lang **andauern.**	A ______ match can ______ for 5 days.
Vor einem Auto**rennen** muss man die **Bremsen** der Autos kontrollieren.	Before a car ______ you must control the ______ of the cars.
Man spielt **Eishockey** auf dem **Eis** und die Spieler benutzen  .	You play ______ on ______ and the players use ______ .

2 A crossword

Find the right solutions.

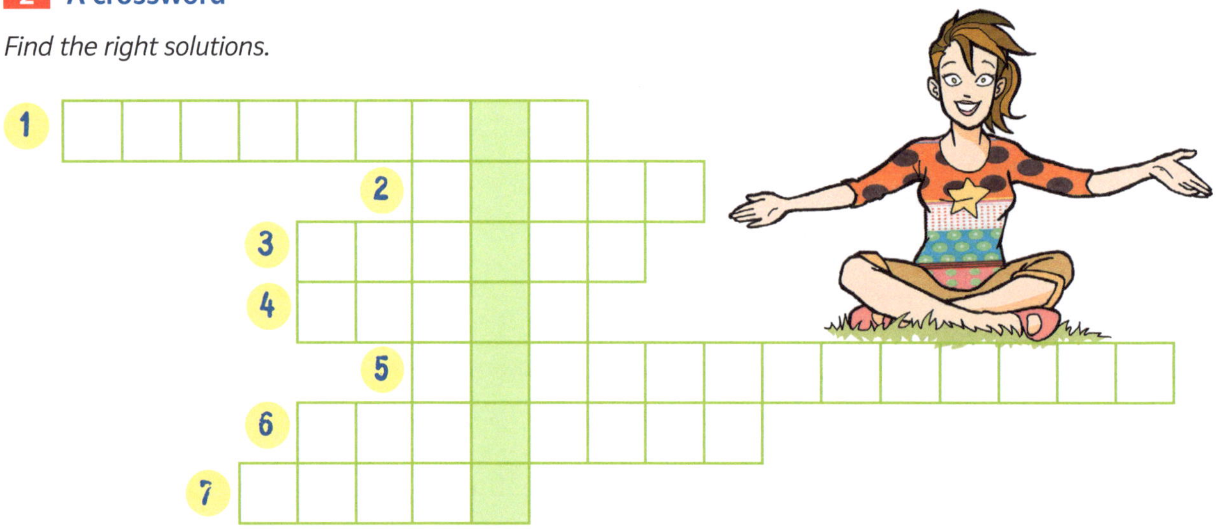

4. another word for football field

1. It is one of the oldest sports in the world.

2. It is usually 400 metres long.

7. It's the place where you play tennis.

3. This person controls a tennis match.

6. In this sport there are four bases on a field.

5. It is like surfing on land. You jump and do tricks in the air.

Solution: A popular sport in Australia, England, India, New Zealand, Pakistan and South Africa:

______

→ pages 10/11

What do you remember?		
Der Skateboard Wettbewerb ist ein großes **Ereignis** für Laura.	The skateboarding competition is a big ____________ for Laura.	☐
Kay hat das **Gefühl**, dass sie gute **Chancen** haben wird.	Kay has the ____________ that she'll have good ____________ .	☐
Der neue Skatepark **eröffnet erst, wenn** der Regen aufhört.	The new skatepark ____________ the rain stops.	☐
Er ist in einer bösen **Situation**.	He is in a bad ____________ .	☐
Hast du **Pläne** für morgen?	Have you made any ____________ for your party yet?	☐

3 Word search

Complete the dialogue with the words you find in the box.

A	U	N	T	I	L	R	B	S	T	Y	R	T	U	S	S	G
E	E	E	R	G	N	O	B	A	E	F	U	R	T	S	G	L
S	V	R	Y	Y	U	M	U	S	I	T	U	A	T	I	O	N
O	T	E	G	T	X	S	J	W	F	G	J	I	X	B	P	E
P	F	F	N	U	H	A	M	E	R	I	C	A	N	R	E	R
C	S	V	D	T	L	X	I	D	X	D	C	O	G	U	N	E
E	D	J	A	R	R	A	N	G	E	M	E	N	T	S	E	W

Mary: "I've made special ____________ for us next weekend."

Jane: "What are you planning?"

Mary: "The new fitness club in Greenwich is going to ____________ on Saturday. They're going to have a big ____________ and they're going to show us new ____________ fitness exercises."

Jane: "Sounds great. But my mum says I can't go out ____________ I finish my Maths homework."

Mary: "Haven't you done that yet? Well, this is a difficult ____________, but I'll help you!"

4 Spot the mistakes

Find two mistakes in each sentence. Underline them and write down the correct version.

1 Please wear a helm for scateboarding. ____________

2 The race don't stop until someone win. ____________

3 Basebal is an american sport. ____________

→ page 12

What do you remember?	
Zustimmen und **Widersprechen** ist wichtig für eine Unterhaltung.	____________ and ____________ is important for a conversation.
to say yes	____________
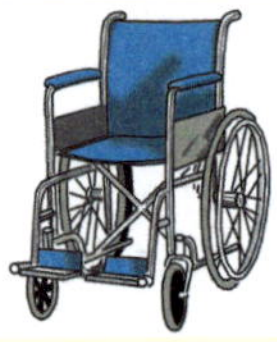	____________
Lies den Text **einmal**.	Read the text ____________ .
Man braucht **Glück** um ein Fußballspiel zu gewinnen.	You need ____________ to win a football match.
Das ist **genau** das, was ich auch denke.	That's ____________ what I think, too.
Nein, das ist **Quatsch**!	No, that's ____________ !

5 Agreeing and disagreeing

Use the phrases from page 12 in your textbook to say if you agree or disagree with the following statements; then give your opinion.

1. "Women don't play football as well as men."
   I don't agree. I think they can play as well as men./I agree.
   Men usually play football better than women.
2. "Cricket is a very boring sport."
   ____
3. "Girls shouldn't play rugby. It's too hard for them."
   ____
4. "When you play sports it's important to have fun, not just to win."
   ____
5. "The referee is always right."
   ____
6. "It's OK to hurt somebody in order to win."
   ____

→ pages 13–15

What do you remember?		
Ein **American Football** Spiel hat zwei **Halbzeiten**.	A match of ______ has got two ______ .	☐
Im Fernsehen ist eine **Werbepause** dazwischen.	On TV, there is a ______ between them.	☐
Kennst du einen **Kanal, der** keine **Werbespots** hat?	Do you know a ______ ______ has no ______ ?	☐
Es ist nicht **ungewöhnlich**, dass Sport**wissenschaftler** zum **Rudern Athleten** mit großen **Lungen** auswählen.	It's not ______ sport ______ choose ______ with big ______ for ______ .	☐
Der Athlet, der die **Goldmedaille** im **Schwimmen** gewann, war **behindert**.	The athlete who won the ______ in ______ was ______ .	☐
Er brach sogar den Welt**rekord**.	He even broke the world ______ .	☐

6 Sport and pictures

Write down the sport that belongs to the picture. Find more words connected to that sport.

	Sport	Football
	Other words	referee,
	Sport	
	Other words	
	Sport	
	Other words	
	Sport	
	Other words	
	Sport	
	Other words	

→ pages 13–15

What do you remember?		
Ein **Relativsatz** ohne **Relativpronomen** heißt …	A ______ without ______ is called ______ .	☐
Cool Runnings ist ein Film, **der** die Geschichte eines **Bob**teams erzählt.	*Cool Runnings* is a film ______ tells the story of a ______ team.	☐
'**zero**' in tennis	______	☐
Athleten, **deren** Lungen groß sind, sind oft gut im Schwimmen.	Athletes ______ lungs are big are often good at swimming.	☐
Nach dem **Marathon** war sein T-Shirt voller **Schweiß**.	After the ______ his T-Shirt was full of ______ .	☐
Peter spielt Tennis und er spielt **auch** Fußball.	Peter plays tennis and he ______ plays football.	☐
	______	☐
Kennst du einige **Kuriositäten** über Sport?	Do you know any ______ about sport?	☐
Manchmal ist es schwierig, die **genaue Definition** eines Wortes zu finden.	Sometimes it's difficult to find the ______ ______ of a word.	☐

7 Definitions

Explain the following words.

1. ______
2. ______
3. ______
4. ______
5. ______
6. ______
7. ______
8. ______

snow
gold medal
commercial break
record
bobsleigh
rowing
to sweat
oddity

→ pages 16–18

What do you remember?		
Skispringen • Tradition • Skispringer • Adler	______ is a sport that has no ______ in England, but in 1988 a British ______ became famous: Eddie the ______ .	☐
Pressekonferenz • Transporter	At a ______ he told the reporters how he slept in a ______ when he went to competitions.	☐
 sich beschlagen • Skibrille	He also had a problem with his ______ . They ______ when he put his ______ over them.	☐
gleiten • flattern • können	He ______ over the snow, jumped and ______ his arms when we was in the air, even if he didn't think he ______ win.	☐
weit • Platz • winken	He jumped only ______ enough for the last ______ , but he was happy and ______ at his fans.	☐

8 An interview with Eddie

After the competition Eddie gives another interview to a reporter. Write down the questions and answers.

Der Reporter fragt Eddie, ob er traurig ist, dass er nicht so weit wie die anderen gesprungen ist.

Reporter: ______________________________

Eddie antwortet, dass es nur gut genug für den letzten Platz war, aber dass er zu den Olympischen Spielen gehen konnte, und dass er deswegen sehr glücklich ist.

Eddie: ______________________________

____

Der Reporter fragt, ob Eddie, als er sprang, irgendwelche Probleme mit seiner Brille hatte.

Reporter: ______________________________

Eddie antwortet, dass sie sich beschlug, als er seine Skibrille aufsetzte.

Eddie: ______________________________

____

Der Reporter bedankt sich für das Interview und wünscht Eddie viel Glück für die Zukunft.

Reporter: ______________________________

→ page 19

What do you remember?	
Wenn man ein Wort benutzt, ist es wichtig, auf den **Kontext** zu schauen.	When you use a word, it is important to look at the ______________________ .

9 What's the context?

German words can have different meanings in English. Look at some different meanings of these German words and write down a sentence for each. Use a dictionary for help.

bitte	please	Could you help me, please?
	You're welcome.	
	pardon	
Seite	side	
	page	
Programm	channel	
	programme	
	range	
	agenda	
erinnern	to remind	
	to remember	

10 Find the right words

A German boy is staying with a guest family in England for two weeks. In the evening he is telling his guest mother about his day, but there are words he doesn't know. Can you help him? Find his ideas in a German-English dictionary.

Turnier • Torwart • Ergebnis • Kartoffelbrei • ägyptische Statuen • Raumschiffe • Außerirdische

We had a football ______________________ at school this morning. I was the ______________________ of my team. The ________________ of the match was nil - nil. I had ______________________ and sausages for lunch. In the afternoon we went to a museum where we saw ______________________ . In the evening we went to the cinema and watched a film about ______________________ and ______________________ .

11 Jumbled words

Put the letters of these sports words into the right order and complete the grid. There are some words that fit more than once.

cei | tab | lavo blal | difel | thelem | sabe | logeggs | katerdosab | tawer | ikcts | eeerfre | wons | logd damel

baseball	swimming	rugby	skateboarding	ice-hockey	ski jump	cricket

12 Words as verbs and nouns

Read the sentences and decide if the marked words are used as verbs (V) or nouns (N).

1. It was a big **surprise** (____) that the athlete won the gold medal.
2. Thank you for your **help** (____).
3. I **hope** (____) there won't be a **queue** (____) for the toilets.
4. She has got many **hopes** (____) and **dreams** (____).
5. It often **rains** (____) in London, but there isn't much **snow** (____) in winter.
6. **Sleep** (____) does not always **help** (____) when you feel bad.
7. He **dreamed** (____) of the gold medal, but he wasn't fast enough.

13 Words that you link

Read the sentences and mark the words that you link with ‿.

1. There‿is an unusual athlete in the competition.
2. Anne ate an apple.
3. He put on his uniform and left.
4. Almost everyone can find a sport that they like.
5. It isn't important to win.
6. I had an accident: I fell off my skateboard!

14 A crossword

Complete the crossword puzzle with the right words. Where the words are already given, you must write clues with relative clauses.

ACROSS	DOWN
1. the place where you play tennis 4. a competition to see who is the fastest 5. a relative pronoun 8. ______ 10. ______ 11. The Olympic Games are a very important … for athletes. 12. A referee …s a football match. 14. sth your parents and grandparents already did 16. In tennis it means 'zero'. 17. If you are happy or if you are angry, you have … 18. ______	2. ______ 3. It is white and we often see it in winter. 4. You hold it in your hand when you play tennis. 6. sth unusual 7. It describes a word. 9. You can put it on your head. 12. ______ 13. ______ 15. It is bigger than a car.

Unit 2 Once upon a time ...

→ pages 24/25

What do you remember?		
Es war einmal ein schönes, aber sehr armes Mädchen.	______________ there was a very poor girl.	☐
Sie wusste nicht, dass sie die **Erbin** eines reichen **Normannen** war.	She didn't know that she was the ______________ of a rich ______________ .	☐
Sie arbeitete für einen **Sachsen** und sie **hasste** es.	She worked for a ______________ and she ______________ it.	☐
Jeden Tag sammelte sie **Holz** für ihn.	Every day she collected ______________ for him.	☐
Eines Tages **griff** ihn ein **Ritter an** und **besiegte** ihn.	One day a ______________ ______________ and ______________ him.	☐
Er sagte (auf Französisch) „**Guten Tag!**" zu dem Mädchen.	He said " ______________ !" to the girl.	☐
Das Mädchen ging mit ihm und bekam viel  .	The girl went with him and got a lot of ______________ .	☐
Dies passierte vor **Jahrhunderten**.	This happened ______________ ago.	☐

1 Scrambled words

Put the letters into the right order and complete the text.

______________ CONE NUOP A EMIT, many ______________ TENCERUIS ago, there was a very rich king. He had a lot of ______________ LOGD, and many ______________ STIGNHK followed him. He had a son who should become his ______________ RIHE, but he ______________ DAHET his father. He ______________ DEACKTAT him and tried to kill him, but the king ______________ DEDEATEF him.

→ pages 24/25

What do you remember?		
 sind meine **Lieblings**tiere.	___ are my ___ animals.	☐
„**Guten Tag meine Kleinen**“, sagte der normannische König.	“___”, the Norman king said.	☐
„**Romeo, Romeo warum musst du nur Romeo sein?**“ ist eine berühmte Phrase von Shakespeare.	“___?” is a famous phrase by Shakespeare.	☐
Im Jahre 43 **nach Christus** kamen die Römer in Großbritannien an.	In the year 43 ___ (= ___) the Romans arrived in Britain.	☐
Sie sagten „**Seid gegrüßt!**“ und „**Es soll Euch gut gehen!**“.	They said “___!” and “___!”.	☐
Sie bauten Hadrian's Wall, um die Schotten **draußen** zu **halten.**	They built Hadrian's Wall to ___ the Scots.	☐
„**Bis später**“, sagte das spanische Mädchen und ging fort.	“___”, said the Spanish girl and went away.	☐

2 Who says what?

Fill in the missing words and put them into the right form where necessary.

century, bonjour, to attack, salve, knight, to keep out, hasta luego, to hate, to defeat

1 

We ___ you in 1588, but you ___ our Armada. ___ !

2 

___ ! This is Hadrian's Wall. It ___ the wild Scots.

3 

___ ! I am a Norman ___ .

For ___ the Saxons ___ us.

→ pages 24/25

What do you remember?	
Elisabeth war **Protestantin** und wollte stärker sein als das **katholische** Spanien.	Elizabeth was a _____ and wanted to be stronger than _____ Spain.
Shakespeare lebte im **elisabethanischen Zeitalter.**	Shakespeare lived in the _____.
Er war ein großer **Dichter.**	He was a great _____.
Die **Dampfmaschine** war eine **Erfindung** der **Industriellen Revolution.**	The _____ was an _____ of the _____.
Großbritannien war die „**Werkstatt** der Welt".	Britain was the "_____ of the world".
Es gab **Strom.**	There was _____.
Viele Menschen arbeiteten in **Stahlfabriken.**	Many people worked in _____.
Nach dem **Zweiten Weltkrieg** wurden die **Kolonien** des Britischen **Reiches unabhängig.**	After _____ the _____ of the British _____ became _____.
Jetzt ist Großbritannien Teil der **Europäischen Union.**	Now Britain is part of the _____.

3 History

Match the following words to their times in history.

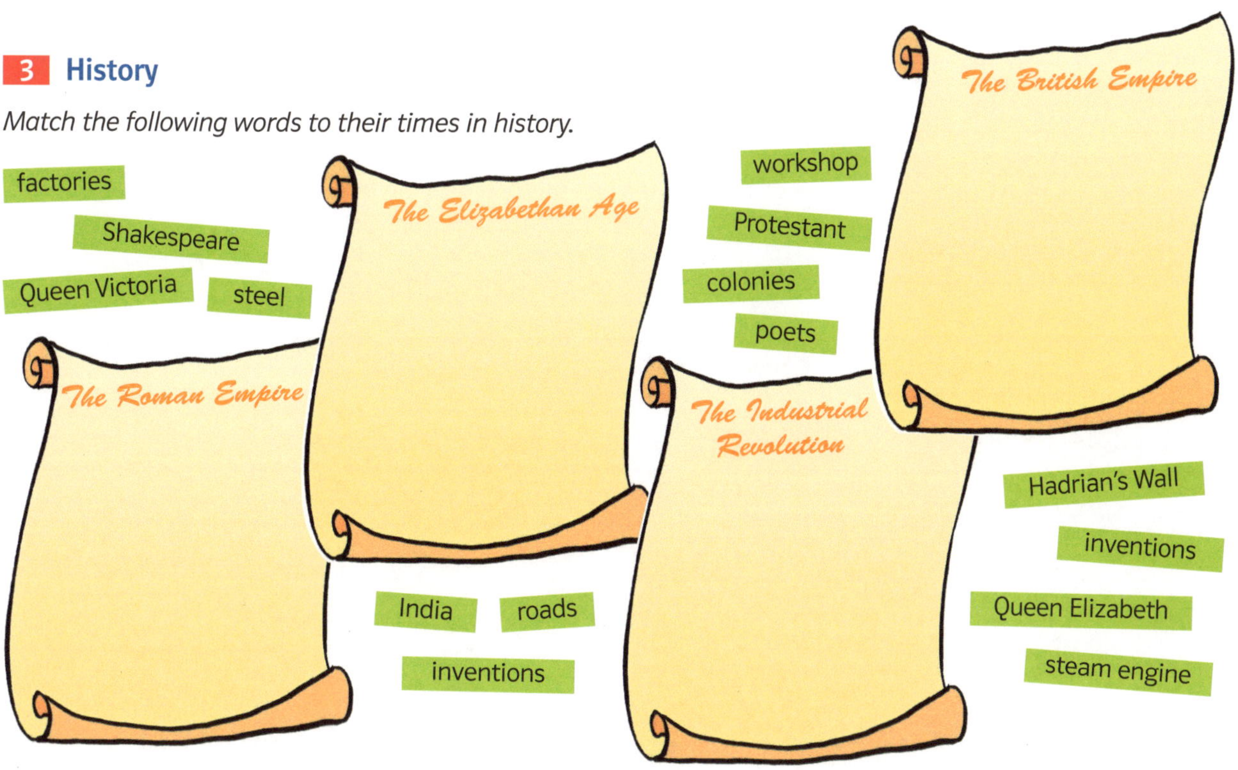

→ pages 26–28

What do you remember?		
Im **Wachs**museum gibt es viele berühmte Leute.	In the ______ museum there are many famous people.	☐
Viele tragen wunderschöne **Kleider**.	Many of them wear beautiful ______ .	☐
Konnte Shakespeare gute Theaterstücke schreiben?	______ Shakespeare ______ write good plays?	☐
Bilde die **Verneinungsform** des **folgenden** Satzes.	Make the ______ of the ______ sentence.	☐
„Ich **darf nicht** ausgehen. Ich **muss** daheim bleiben." – „**Was?!**"	"I ______ go out. I ______ stay at home." – "______ !"	☐
Die **Handlung** des Theaterstücks passiert auf der **Bühne**.	The ______ in the play happens on ______ .	☐
Königin Elizabeth war eine **moderne** Frau.	Queen Elizabeth was a ______ woman.	☐
Briten sind Menschen aus Großbritannien.	______ are people from Britain.	☐

4 Modal auxiliaries and their substitutes

Put in the right modal auxiliary or substitute. Use the right tense.

1. "At first I ______ play the guitar well enough and ______ practise a lot."
2. Ben ______ go on holiday with his friends next year. His parents promised him.
3. Lisa ______ go to the disco last night. It was too late.

5 How to visit a museum

You visit a museum and talk to the staff. What do you say in the following situations?

1. Du möchtest wissen, ob Schüler weniger für die Eintrittskarten zahlen.

______

2. Du fragst, wo du ein Andenken kaufen kannst.

______

3. Du findest den Raum über das Britische Reich nicht.

______

→ page 29

What do you remember?		
Die Schule plant einen **Tag der offenen Tür**.	The school is planning an ______ .	☐
Habt ihr irgendwelche **Vorschläge**?	Do you have any ______ ?	☐
Vorschläge machen ist sehr wichtig.	______ is very important.	☐
Lasst uns Abendessen für die Gäste **zubereiten**.	Let's ______ dinner for the guests.	☐
Der Koch **schlug vor**, Spaghetti zu machen.	The cook ______ to make spaghetti.	☐
Ich denke, wir **sollten** etwas Anderes machen.	I think we ______ make something else.	☐

6 Making suggestions

An exchange student from England is staying with you. Together with your parents you are making plans.

Dein Vater fragt dich, ob du irgendwelche Vorschläge hast, was ihr ihm zeigen könntet.

Your dad: "______"

Du möchtest ihm das Stadtzentrum zeigen. Du denkst, ihr könntet den Bus dorthin nehmen.

You: "______"

Deine Mutter meint, ihr solltet das Museum über deutsche Geschichte besuchen.

Your mum: "______"

Sie schlägt vor, dass du im Internet nach den Eintrittspreisen schaust.

Your mum: "______"

Dein Vater hält das für eine gute Idee; er meint, du könntest dort aber auch anrufen.

Your dad: "______"

7 Find the word

Find out which word is described here.

1. It is a big grey animal. ______
2. Our computers, TVs and lights need it. ______
3. It is a day on which you can visit something and get information. ______
4. It is something which usually only women wear. ______
5. It is the French word for 'hello'. ______

→ pages 30/31

What do you remember?

Was war im **viktorianischen** England **gefragt**?	What was "______" in ______ England?
Der Tower of London wurde früher als **Gefängnis** benutzt.	In the past, the Tower of London was used as a ______ .
1877 wurde Königin Victoria **Kaiserin** von Indien.	In 1877 Queen Victoria became ______ of India.
Ihre **Herrschaft** war sehr lang.	Her ______ was very long.
Sie verbrachte über 63 Jahre auf dem  .	She spent more than 63 years on the ______ .
Sie bekam **Rohstoffe** von ihren Kolonien.	She got ______ from her colonies.
Eine **Festung** hat oft **Türme**.	A ______ has often got ______ .
Jetzt kenne ich das **Plusquamperfekt**!	Now I know the ______ !
Bis 1870 gab es keine **kostenlosen** Schulen und Kinder von **Farmern** mussten arbeiten.	Until 1870 there were no ______ schools, and children of ______ had to work.
Sie lebten oft in **Slums** und schliefen auf dem **Boden**, der nicht **sauber** war.	They often lived in ______ and slept on the ______ , which was not ______ .
Die **Regierung** half ihnen nicht.	The ______ didn't help them.

8 Lost vowels

In these sentences the vowels of some words are lost. Can you put them in?

1. The g__v__rnm__nt made the s__gg__st____n that f__rm__rs should get more money.
2. The __ct____n in Shakespeare's plays happened on st__g__ .
3. In the V__ctor____n age Queen Victoria was on the thr__n__ and she was also __mpr__ss of India.

→ page 32

What do you remember?		
Bereite dich auf das Lesen einer Geschichte **vor**!	________________ to read a story!	☐
Wovon **handelt** der Text?	What __________ the text __________ ?	☐
Schau dir das Bild als Aktivität **vor dem Lesen** an!	Look at the picture as a ______________ activity!	☐
Finde zuerst das **Wesentliche** heraus und dann die **Details**.	First find out the ______________ and then the ______________ .	☐
Wie **hängen** die Figuren zusammen?	How __________ the characters __________ ?	☐
Schau **genau** hin und ziehe eine **Verbindungslinie**!	Take a ______________ look and draw a ______________ .	☐

9 Reading activities

When can you do the following activities? Complete the grid.

read the story slowly • guess who the characters could be • look at the pictures • make a list of interesting words • look at the title • read the story quickly • guess what the story could be about • compare the different characters • look up important words • find out the most important ideas • find headings for the different parts

Pre-reading	First reading	Second reading	A closer look

→ pages 33–35

What do you remember?		
Bedienstete • Frau • ernähren	In 1878 Gwendolyn worked as a ______________ in ______________ Cumberland's house. She had to help to ______________ her brothers and sisters.	☐
einsam	She was very ______________ at first, but then she found a friend – Timothy.	☐
sechster Sinn • merkwürdige Visionen	He had the ______________ and so he often had ______________.	☐
den Brunnen putzen • Seltsames	While he was ______________, he saw something ______________: Mrs Lacy had fallen into it.	☐
ertrinken	He also saw other things, like a man who had ______________.	☐
solche • Freundin • wer auch immer • wo auch immer	______________ visions were horrible. One vision showed that Clarence and his ______________ Chloe, ______________ they were and ______________ they were, would have an accident:	☐
Metall Flug-	Their ______________ machine would fall from the air.	☐
keine Ahnung haben	Gwendolyn and Timothy ______________ how to help them.	☐

10 Odd word out

Find the word that does not fit and cross it out.

1. farmer • Catholic • poet • servant
2. girlfriend • mother • sister • grandmother
3. lonely • sad • exciting • boring
4. must • can • go • need

11 Bits and pieces

Form 12 words with these syllables. Write them down on the lines.

pre- -son -vant -sion -pare -tail -tion -press ac- vi- de- far- ser- lone- pri- -mer mo- -wer em- -ly po- foun- -dern -tain

______________ ______________ ______________ ______________

______________ ______________ ______________ ______________

______________ ______________ ______________ ______________

→ pages 33–35

What do you remember?	
lady ≠	____________
altmodisch • Schmuck	The lady wore ____________ ____________ .
tief Luft holen • Telegramm	The servant ____________ when he read the ____________ .
eigentlich • 	____________ , he looked as if he had seen a ____________ .
sich fragen • scherzen	He ____________ if somebody was ____________ .
antworten	So he didn't ____________ .

12 Opposites

Find the opposites of the following words.

1. girlfriend • ____________
2. to love • ____________
3. lady • ____________
4. dirty • ____________
5. detail • ____________
6. odd • ____________
7. to close • ____________
8. modern • ____________
9. to ask • ____________

13 Crossword puzzle

Fill in the crossword.

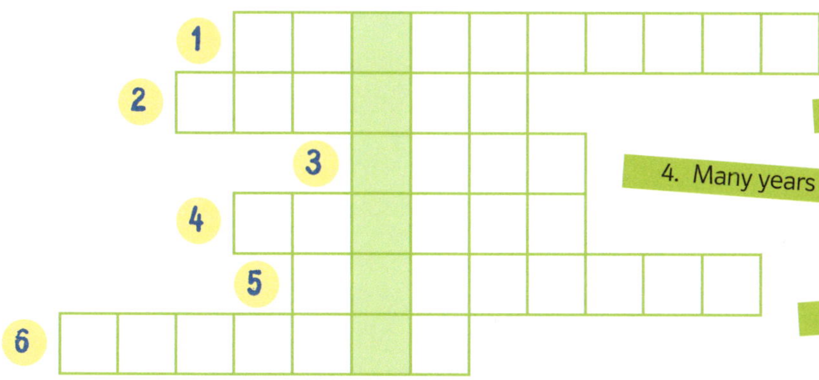

5. You can get water from a …

4. Many years ago the Tower of London was a …

1. It controls a country.

6. Every lord and lady had a … who helped them in the house and in the garden.

2. The British … made Britain very rich because it had many colonies then.

3. Many poor people lived there at the time of the Industrial Revolution.

Solution: People who have ____________s might have the sixth sense.

→ pages 33–35

What do you remember?	
Paragraph • Ende	The ___ had a sad ___ .
to stop ≠	___
Klicken • Leitung	There was a ___ in the ___ .
 mother  grandmother  great grandmother	 ___
neugierig • scheinen	When she woke up she was ___ if the sun was ___ .
nicken	He agreed and ___ .
 Laura Catherine Brown	Catherine is her ___ .

14 Synonyms

Replace the marked word with a word or expression with the same meaning.

1. "Are you hungry?" Cindy asked. "No, I'm not. I've just had a sandwich," Billy **answered** (➜ ___).
2. Carry: "All my friends are on holiday, so I feel **alone** (➜ ___)".
3. I always have an **odd** (➜ ___) feeling when something bad is going to happen.
4. In 2008 Jerry went on holiday to Italy. But **the next** (➜ ___) year he went to Scotland.
5. Teacher: "Ben, please **go on** (➜ ___)."
6. Lady Cumberland's son **died in the water** (➜ ___).

15 Spot the mistakes

Find three mistakes in every sentence and write the correct version down.

1 Bens great-great-mother nodded after she had listen to the details.

___

2 E-mails are moderner than telegramms and they are also more fast.

___

→ page 36

What do you remember?	
Betone die wichtigen Wörter im Satz.	________________ the important words in the sentence.
Was ist die richtige **Betonung**?	What is the right ________________ ?

16 French words in English

Jacques uses some French words when he is talking. Underline them and write the English words down.

Last Saturday I visited my famille in Paris. The départ of my plane was at 9.30 am and I had to changer the plane once. At the airport my grands-parents and my cousin waited for me. They were very happy to have me as their visiteur. In the evening we went to the théâtre. There was a very good acteur.

________________ ________________ ________________ ________________

________________ ________________ ________________ ________________

17 Word search

There are ten English words of French origin in the box. Find them and write them down.

G	F	C	A	D	I	F	F	E	R	E	N	T	B	R	E	M	P
E	E	D	I	A	L	O	G	U	E	Z	B	Y	D	F	M	X	R
C	A	D	F	G	H	U	T	V	H	Z	O	U	G	D	U	C	O
H	I	S	T	O	R	Y	X	G	A	C	T	I	O	N	S	R	B
R	V	T	I	U	R	C	B	Z	A	D	T	S	V	E	I	V	L
M	U	Y	Y	A	S	E	F	B	N	M	L	D	A	N	C	E	E
A	S	C	V	B	R	O	C	H	U	R	E	F	B	T	M	M	M

____

____

____

18 Sentence stress

Find the important words in these sentences and underline them. Read the sentences out loud.

1. The poet William Shakespeare lived in the Elizabethan Age and wrote the famous play Romeo and Juliet.
2. In the 18th century there was the Industrial Revolution, a time of many inventions like the steam engine.
3. The British Empire was the age when Britain had many colonies and Queen Victoria was on the throne.

19 Crossword puzzle

Find the right solutions.

ACROSS	DOWN

ACROSS

2. Madame Tussauds is a … museum.
4. You don't have to pay for it. It's …
5. The time of Queen Elizabeth is the Elizabethan …
8. In a sentence the … lies on important words.
10. It is quite expensive and you can make jewellery of it.
11. a dirty place where very poor people live
13. a place where workers make things
14. the opposite of the gist
15. The sun …s by day.
16. 'wasn't' is the … of 'was'.
17. If you see things that are going to happen in the future you have a …
18. The steam engine was an important …
19. Someone who wants to know everything is …

DOWN

1. the short form of favourite
3. the person who gets another person's money after he or she has died
6. Sometimes when you are shocked, you …
7. William Shakespeare was a …
9. the Victorian Age = The British …
12. the opposite of old-fashioned
13. a building with strong walls and towers

Revision Unit 1 + 2

1 Scrambled words: People

Put the letters into the right order to find people you learnt about in Units 1 and 2. Then write down definitions.

1.	PERIUM		
2.	TAHOCLIC		
3.	TEPO		
4.	MANRICAE		
5.	THINKG		
6.	LETAHET		
7.	PRESESM		
8.	EHIR		
9.	MARFER		
10.	STANERV		
11.	DYLA		
12.	NISTCETIS		

2 Word search

Find 20 words from Units 1 and 2 in the box and write them down on the lines.

G	K	R	A	T	D	H	F	U	B	A	S	E	D	J	O	K	E	N
A	Q	M	A	R	A	T	H	O	N	O	N	O	A	R	N	B	B	F
S	A	G	R	E	E	I	N	G	G	E	G	D	W	R	C	F	B	C
P	C	L	W	D	V	M	O	F	X	J	O	D	E	F	E	A	T	U
A	T	D	S	G	V	Y	D	F	H	K	E	K	L	L	P	U	Y	R
T	U	S	C	W	F	S	S	S	S	P	A	S	V	A	I	D	G	I
A	A	O	V	O	E	A	T	P	O	W	E	R	D	P	D	N	M	O
X	L	O	L	N	E	V	G	Z	J	E	E	G	H	J	K	B	E	U
D	L	U	O	D	D	I	T	Y	D	A	O	A	F	C	B	T	B	S
F	Y	X	U	E	C	D	R	G	H	J	U	M	T	B	T	R	X	I
E	A	V	O	R	C	T	E	L	E	G	R	A	M	K	O	P	E	N

Unit 3 Living together

→ pages 42/43

What do you remember?	
Sam and Lewis sind **Zwillinge**.	Sam and Lewis are ___ .
Lewis **benimmt sich** manchmal sehr schlecht.	Lewis sometimes ___ very badly.
Er **räumt** nie sein Zimmer **auf**.	He never ___ his room.
Die **Putzfrau** ist sehr böse, wenn sie das Durcheinander sieht.	The ___ is very angry when she sees the mess Lewis has made.
„Der Junge **macht mich verrückt**," sagt sie zu Lewis' Mutter.	"That boy ___ ," she tells his mother.
Sam und Lewis **verstehen sich** gut.	Sam and Lewis ___ well.
Sie helfen **sich** oft **gegenseitig** bei den Hausaufgaben.	They often help ___ with their homework.
Sam ist **Vegetarier**, aber Lewis isst gerne Fleisch.	Sam is a ___ , but Lewis likes meat.
Er findet, einige Gemüsesorten sind OK, aber er hasst **Rosenkohl**.	He likes some vegetables, but he hates ___ .
Seine Eltern sagen ihm oft, „**Iss** dein Gemüse **auf**."	His parents often tell him, " ___ your vegetables."
Aber er sagt, „Nein, danke" und schiebt eine in die **Mikrowelle**. 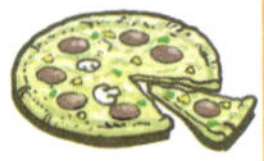	But he says, "No thanks" – and puts a ___ pizza in the ___ .

1 Which words go together?

Write down the correct word or words.

crazy · a suggestion · the way · lost · curly · a lie · fun · his teeth · lucky · the shopping

1. Jamie's hair has gone ___ .
2. Hannah won a prize. – She was ___ .
3. Pete says he has never told ___ .
4. Mark's questions drive me ___ .
5. Alex always has ___ at the weekend.
6. I would like to make ___ .
7. Louise can find ___ alone.
8. Rob must brush ___ .
9. Don't get ___ in town.
10. Max is going to do ___ .

→ pages 42/43

What do you remember?		
Norman liebte Louisa und wollte sie **heiraten**.	Norman loved Louisa and wanted to ______ her.	☐
Jeden Tag hinterließ er Mitteilungen auf ihrem **Anrufbeantworter**.	Every day he left messages on her ______ .	☐
Aber eines Tages **trennten sie sich**.	But one day they ______ .	☐
Louisa sagte zu Norman, „Ich will dich **nicht mehr** sehen."	Louisa told Norman, "I don't want to see you ______ ."	☐
Das war **Pech** für Norman.	That was ______ for Norman.	☐
Er dachte: „Ich war nicht sehr **klug**.	He thought: "I wasn't very ______ .	☐
Louisa ist ein sehr **selbstsüchtiges** Mädchen.	Louisa is a very ______ girl.	☐
Aber **das ist mir egal**. Sie ist nicht das einzige Mädchen.	But ______ . She isn't the only girl.	☐
Ich muss irgendwo ein nettes Mädchen **kennenlernen**, **sonst** werde ich einsam sein."	I must ______ a nice girl somewhere, ______ I'll be lonely."	☐
Als Norman im **Heimwerkerladen** war, sah er ein schönes Mädchen.	When Norman was in the ______ , he saw a beautiful girl.	☐
Sie trug einen coolen  .	She was wearing a cool sun ______ .	☐
Er überlegte: „Soll ich sie nach ihrer **Telefonnummer** fragen?"	He thought: "Shall I ask her for her ______ number?"	☐

2 Sounds

Mark the words that you link. Look at the example.

1. Nina told a lie when she spoke to Frank at the party.
2. Eat up your burger, then we'll find out about the concert.
3. The kids get on well with their parents, but they don't agree about food or music.
4. I often look at TV programmes about interesting people.
5. George always makes his own pizzas and shares them with his old friend Andy.
6. Danny spends almost all his pocket money on expensive computer games or DVDs.

→ pages 42/43

What do you remember?	
Eine **von** drei Familien in der Stadt hat einen Garten.	One ______ three families in the Wilsons' town has a garden.
Viele Bäume **wachsen** in ihrem Garten.	Lots of trees ______ in their garden.
Man kann einen Baum von einem Apfel**kern** bekommen.	You can get a tree from an apple ______ .
Sue isst jeden Morgen ein Sandwich, aber sie wirft die **Kruste** weg.	Sue has a sandwich every morning, but she throws away the ______ .
Nach dem Frühstück **putzt sich** Sue immer **die** 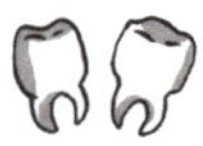 .	Sue always ______ after breakfast.
Wenn sie in den Regen hinausgeht, **kräuseln sich** ihre Haare.	When she goes out in the rain, her hair ______ .
Sue und Emily sind beste Freundinnen, und sie **lügen** nie.	Sue and Emily are best friends, and they never ______ .
Sie schicken sich oft gegenseitig SMS. Sue schreibt: „Bin ich **zu spät** für den Film im Fernsehen?“	They often send texts to each other. Sue writes: “Am I ______ for the TV film?”
Emily antwortet: „Nein **du bist** OK.“	Emily replies: “No, ______ OK.”
Sie sitzen oft zusammen und schauen sich **Szenen** aus ihren Lieblingsfilmen an.	They often sit together and watch ______ from their favourite films.

3 A puzzle

Write down the words.

1 another word for “clever”
2 You should brush them every day.
3 When it's very cold, water is …
4 Vegetarians don't eat it.
5 You can wear one of these on your head.
6 People think Friday 13th brings bad …
7 You can leave messages on an answer…

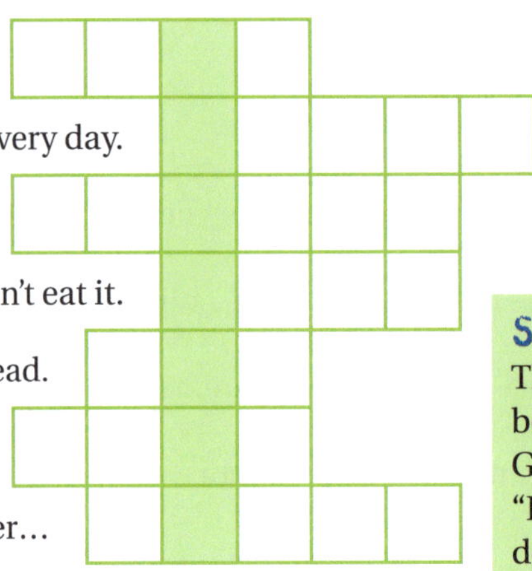

Solution
The letters in the green boxes make a word. – Grandpa Patterson says: “Be careful with pips. You don't want a tree in your ______ !”

→ pages 44/45

What do you remember?	
Richard schreibt die Songs für seine Band **selbst**.	Richard writes the songs for his band ______________.
Letzten Freitag haben sie ein Konzert in einem **Altersheim** gegeben.	Last Friday they gave a concert in an ______________.
Sie hatten sich **entschieden**, Songs zu spielen, die nicht zu laut waren.	They had ______________ to play songs which were not too loud.
Der Saal war voll, und man musste **mehr** Stühle holen.	The hall was full, and people had to get ______________ chairs.
Am Anfang fühlte sich Richard nervös, aber dann begann er, **sich** zu **entspannen**.	Richard felt nervous at first, but then he began to ______________.
„Die alten Leute **hatten** echt **Spaß**," sagte er später.	"The old people really ______________," he said later.
„Ich war überrascht, weil mein Vater meine Musik nicht **ausstehen** kann.	"I was surprised because my dad can't ______________ my music.
Wenn ich gerade Songs höre, sagt er oft, ‚Kannst du die Musik bitte **abstellen**.'"	When I'm listening to songs, he often says, 'Can you ______________ that music ______________, please.'"

4 With or without '-self' / '-selves'?

Put in the right word.

you / yourself · me / myself · you / yourselves · us / ourselves · it / itself · them / themselves · us / ourselves · me / myself · him / himself

The girls are thirsty after basketball training, so they often buy ______________ drinks at the snack bar. "Look at my foot," Jenny says. "I hurt ______________ when I fell over. I had a bike accident yesterday. But a nice woman helped ______________. My parents said, 'We'll buy ______________ a new bike for your birthday. – But be more careful!'" "Parents!" Amy answers. "I'm sure we can look after ______________, but parents just don't agree." Then Jenny's mobile rings. "Oh. – Didn't I switch ______________ off?" The caller is her friend Martin. He isn't enjoying ______________ at home. She tells Martin: "We're having fun here. Come and sit with ______________." Thirty minutes later Martin arrives. "Hi, girls. You seem to be enjoying ______________." "Yes, we are. We're glad you're here!"

→ page 44/45

What do you remember?	
Sonntags **ruft** Kelly ihre Freunde **an**, sobald sie aufgewacht ist.	On Sundays Kelly ____________ her friends as soon as she wakes up.
Sie **zieht sich** meistens um 10 Uhr **an**.	She usually ____________ at 10 o'clock.
In der Küche **bedient sie sich** mit Cornflakes.	In the kitchen she ____________ to cornflakes.
Dann fragt sie: „Wo ist der Kaffee? Und der Toast? Muss ich mich um **mich selbst** kümmern?"	Then she asks, "Where's the coffee? And the toast? Must I look after ____________?"
„Ja, warum nicht?" fragt ihre Mutter. „Das Frühstück macht **sich** nicht **selbst**, weißt du."	"Yes, why not?" her mother asks. "Breakfast doesn't make ____________, you know."
Wenn Kelly am Nachmittag zu ihrer Oma geht, ruft ihre Mutter, „Tschüss, Kelly. – Benimm **dich**!"	When Kelly goes to her grandma's house in the afternoon, her mother calls, "Bye, Kelly. – Behave ____________!"

5 Dialogues

Put in the right reflexive pronoun.

1. "Sheila, help us to tidy our room, please!" – "OK. But you should really tidy it ____________."
2. "I can hear Jack's voice. Has he got visitors?" – "I don't think so. Maybe he's talking to ____________."
3. "Now, boys, I'll show you how to cook Brussels sprouts." – "We can do that ____________, Mum."
4. "What did the Schmidts buy?" – "They got a book for a friend and three DVDs for ____________."
5. "You're a fantastic cook, Danny!" – "Thanks. But I didn't teach ____________. I had a good teacher."

6 What did they do?

Find the right sentence for each picture and write down the number.

1. They helped each other.
2. They looked at each other.
3. They looked at themselves.
4. They gave each other presents.
5. They looked after each other.
6. They hurt themselves.
7. They shouted at each other.
8. They gave themselves presents.
9. They helped themselves.

→ page 46

What do you remember?		
Oft leiht sich Linda Sachen von ihrer Schwester aus, und Rachel **hat** meistens **nichts dagegen**.	Linda often borrows her sister's clothes, and Rachel doesn't usually ______ .	☐
Wenn Linda sie zu lange behält, sagt Rachel: „Es gibt einen **Unterschied** zwischen Leihen und Stehlen."	When Linda keeps them too long, Rachel says: "There is a ______ between borrowing and stealing."	☐
Dann **bedauert** Linda ihre Schwester Rachel.	Then Linda ______ her sister Rachel.	☐
Sie arbeitet hart, um Geld für ihre schöne Kleidung zu **verdienen**.	She works hard to ______ money for her nice clothes.	☐
„**Ich verstehe**," sagt Linda. „Es tut mir leid."	" ______ ," Linda says. "I'm sorry."	☐
Manchmal sagt Linda verärgert, „Du räumst deine Sachen nie auf!" – „Hm, **da ist was dran**. Ich werde versuchen, ordentlich zu sein."	Sometimes Linda says angrily, "You never put your things away!" – "Hm, ______ . I'll try to be tidy."	☐
„OK, gut," sagt Linda. „Es ist toll wenn wir uns **entgegenkommen**."	"OK, fine," Linda says."It's great when we ______ ."	☐

7 Meeting halfway

In this dialogue Phil is very aggressive. Write new, more polite sentences for him. Use the notes.

Max: Sorry, Phil, I can't come to the cinema with you this evening.
Phil: No, you can't break a promise! No way!

sad – why not?

____

Max: I can't help it. Mum is working late and I must look after Jimmy.
Phil: Your selfish family! And what about me? I want to go out!

see – problem; alternative?

____

Max: I've got an idea. Maybe we could go another day.
Phil: No, I want to go today. I can't stand people who change their plans!

good idea – tomorrow?

____

Max: Just a moment, Phil. I'll call Mum and ask if I'm free tomorrow.
Phil: Forget it. I'm going to the cinema today!

OK – say yes!

____

→ pages 47/48

What do you remember?		
Scott ist **wahrscheinlich** der Einzige in seiner Klasse mit seinem eigenen Büro.	Scott is ____________ the only person in his class with his own office.	☐
Seine Mitschüler sind sehr **neidisch**.	His school friends are very ____________ of him.	☐
Sein Zimmer ist voller **Gerümpel**.	His bedroom is full of ____________ .	☐
Scotts Eltern **wünschen**, er würde sein Schlafzimmer aufräumen.	Scott's parents ____________ he would tidy up his bedroom.	☐
Scott hat versprochen, seine alten Komikhefte **loszuwerden**.	Scott has promised to ____________ his old comics.	☐
Aber nun hat Scott den Gartenschuppen **in** sein Büro **verwandelt**.	But now Scott has ____________ the garden shed ____________ his office.	☐
Er ist der **Typ** Mensch, der manchmal gerne allein ist.	He's the ____________ of person who likes to be alone sometimes.	☐
Aber er **chattet** gerne mit Leuten online, **besonders** wenn er sein Französisch üben kann.	But he likes to ____________ with people online, ____________ when he can practise his French.	☐
Manchmal darf sein Bruder Rob auch dabei sein, wenn Scott **im Chat** ist.	Sometimes his brother Rob is allowed to be there, too, when Scott is ____________ .	☐
Scott muss die Mitteilungen von seinen französischen Freunden **übersetzen**.	Scott has to ____________ the messages from his French friends.	☐
Rob bittet seinen Bruder oft um **Rat**.	Rob often asks his brother for ____________ .	☐

8 Odd word out

Which word does not fit in? Cross it out and explain your decision.

1. sad • jealous • wise • angry ____________
2. purse • vegetarian • cleaning lady • assistant ____________
3. to wish • to decide • to feel • to brush ____________
4. advice • junk • suggestion • tip ____________
5. purse • comma • pocket • bag ____________

→ page 49

What do you remember?	
David sagte zu Susan, „Jake hat viele Freundinnen“, aber sie **hörte nicht auf** ihn.	David told Susan: “Jake has lots of girlfriends,” but she ______________________ him.
Sie erzählte jedem, „Jake ist mein **Freund**.	She told everybody: “Jake is my ______________________ .
Er möchte nicht mit anderen Mädchen **ausgehen**.“	He doesn’t want to ______________ with any other girls.”
Aber dann hörte sie von Jakes **heimlichen** Telefongesprächen mit ihrer eigenen Schwester.	But then she heard about Jake’s ______________________ phone calls with her own sister.
Als Susan wusste, dass es stimmte, **drehte sie durch**.	When Susan knew it was true, she ______________________ .
„Was kann ich tun?“ dachte sie. „Vielleicht schreibe ich an eine **Kummerkastentante**.“	“What can I do?” she thought. “Maybe I’ll write to an ______________________ .”

9 The wrong word

One word in each sentence is wrong. Underline it and write the correct word on the line.

1. Richard often goes angry when people laugh at teenagers. ______________
2. “Older people make mistakes, too,” he says. “What’s the different?” ______________
3. Richard thinks teenagers should try to sort over their own problems. ______________
4. Richard’s parents sometimes play crazy when he doesn’t take their advice. ______________
5. Every day Richard brings all his free time at the sports club. ______________
6. “I want I could be friends with a cool girl like Anita,” he says. ______________
7. “But she’s going away with that idiot William. ______________
8. Maybe they’ll spell up soon.” ______________

10 Tongue-twisters

Add the missing letters. Then read the tongue-twisters as quickly as you can.

“r” or “l”?

___ed ___o___y,

ye___ ___ow ___o___y

a sheikh [ʃeɪk]

“s” or “sh”?

The ___ick

___eikh’s ___ixth

___eep’s ___ick.

→ page 50

What do you remember?		
Manchmal ist derjenige, den du sprechen willst, **nicht da** oder kann **den Anruf** nicht **entgegennehmen**.	Sometimes the person you want to speak to ____________ or can't ____________ .	☐
Eine unbekannte Stimme sagt, „Harold ist **leider** nicht zu Hause. **Hinterlasse** eine Nachricht auf dem Anrufbeantworter."	A strange voice says, " ____________ Harold isn't at home. ____________ a message on the answerphone."	☐
Du musst auf den **Signalton** warten, dann kannst du sprechen.	You must wait for the ____________ , then you can speak.	☐
Manche **Anrufer** mögen keine Anrufbeantworter oder **Voicemail**.	Some ____________ don't like answerphones or ____________ .	☐
Sie finden es **schwierig**, mit einer Maschine zu sprechen.	They find it ____________ to talk to a machine.	☐
Aber sie können Leute per E-Mail **erreichen**.	But they can ____________ people via e-mail.	☐

11 A phone call

You want to meet your friend James at the sports club on Friday. He isn't in when you call, but you talk to his sister Ruby. Write down what you say. Use the phrases on the right and your own ideas.

Ruby: Hello, this is Ruby Johnson here.

You: Hello. ____________ .

Ruby: I'm afraid James isn't in at the moment.

You: ____________ ?

Ruby: Yes, of course you can. What should I tell him?

You: ____________ .

Ruby: OK, I've got that. What about the time?

You: ____________ .

Ruby: OK. Shall I ask James to phone you back?

You: ____________ .

Ruby: Yes, I'll do that. I've written it down. Bye!

You: ____________ .

I'd like …

… leave message

… tell him that …

… at … o'clock …

… phone me at 0788 …

→ pages 51–53

What do you remember?		
ganz alleine	Tom was a newspaper reporter and he liked to work ______ .	☐
schaffen	But he didn't always ______ to do this.	☐
schlecht gelaunt	When he made a mistake, he was usually ______ .	☐
Halt die Klappe • anbieten	He said " ______ " to people when they ______ to help him.	☐
allein zu Hause • Türklingel	But one day he was ______ when somebody rang his ______ .	☐
Was ist denn hier los?	" ______ ?" he asked when he opened the door.	☐
Typ	Outside he saw Jake, a ______ from his newspaper.	☐
Gespräch	"Tom," Jake said, "we must have a ______ ."	☐
das Wichtigste zuerst	" ______ ", Tom answered. "Why are you here?"	☐
eins nach dem anderen	"To help you. You should think about problems ______ .	☐
sichergehen	And you should ______ that you do the most important job first."	☐
im Weg stehen	"I try," Tom said, "but other people often ______ ."	☐
eine Entscheidung treffen	"Tom, you must ______ ," Jake said. "Work alone and make mistakes, or learn to work in a team."	☐

12 Word pairs

Find pairs of words which sound the same. (You don't need all the words.)

nose · threw · weak · ear · meet · through · sign · seen · news · week · meat · might · knows · hour · our · scene · work · throw

1. nose ______ • ______
2. ______ • ______
3. ______ • ______
4. ______ • ______
5. ______ • ______
6. ______ • ______

→ pages 51–53

What do you remember?

aufführen	It's great fun to ______________ a play.	☐
Schauspielerinnen	There's something to do for everyone, not only for actors and ______________ .	☐
Ensemble	All the people who act in a play are the ______________ .	☐
Kostüme	They often have to wear strange or funny ______________ .	☐
	Some people want to be a hero, others want to be a monster or a ______________ .	☐
Maske	If an actor wants to hide his face, he wears a ______________ .	☐
Requisiten	It's fun to look for all the ______________ for a play – chairs, bottles, toys, …	☐
Beleuchtung	It's dark in a theatre, so you need good ______________ for the stage.	☐
proben	If you want your play to be perfect, you must ______________ it.	☐
Probe	The last ______________ is very important.	☐
Publikum	The people who come to see the play are the ______________ .	☐
Programmheft	Before the play starts, they can read about it in the ______________ .	☐
Vorhang	Then the ______________ goes up and the play begins.	☐
applaudieren	It's a great moment when everybody ______________ at the end.	☐

13 Jumbled words: People and plays

Put the letters in the right order and write down the words.

1. ATSC cast
2. STCAESR ______________
3. HOTURA ______________
4. SHLAARERE ______________
5. NEEDCAIU ______________
6. ROREITDC ______________
7. ORTAC ______________
8. MARMERGOP ______________

14 Find the right pronoun

Underline the right pronoun in each sentence.

1. While Scott and Joey were out on their bikes, Scott fell off and hurt (**him** • **them** • **himself**).
2. "I'll take (**you** • **myself** • **yourself**) to hospital," Joey said.
3. "No, it's OK," Scott said. "I can look after (**me** • **you** • **myself**), thanks.
4. Let's go on with our trip. – We're really enjoying (**me** • **us** • **ourselves**)."
5. But Scott's bike was broken, so they had to push (**it** • **them** • **themselves**) all the way home.
6. In the kitchen Dad was busy. "Will you help (**me** • **you** • **yourselves**) to make the salad?" he asked.
7. Soon the food was ready, and the boys helped (**them** • **himself** • **themselves**).
8. After the meal Dad said, "Oh, your bike. – Let's take (**him** • **it** • **itself**) to the garage. It isn't an official bike shop, but they can mend everything there (**them** • **itself** • **themselves**)."

15 Reflexive in German, not in English

Put in the right English verb. Choose from the German verbs in the box.

sich beeilen · sich entscheiden · sich entspannen · sich anstellen · sich verstecken · sich bewegen · sich erinnern

1. I know that actress's face, but I can't ________________ her name.
2. Who should play the role of the hero – John or Will? The director can't ________________ .
3. In one scene an actress has to ________________ in a cupboard when the monster comes.
4. Andy is playing the role of a tree, so he mustn't ________________ . – He must stand there like a rock.
5. It's 6 o'clock already! We'll be late for the rehearsal if we don't ________________ !
6. Actors often feel nervous, so they try to ________________ before the play begins.
7. If you want to see the play, you'll have to ________________ at the office to buy tickets.

16 Stress the subject

Finish the answers to the questions. Use a reflexive pronoun to stress the subject.

1. "How did you find out about Mary's accident?" – "She told me ________________ ."
2. "Where did you find those fantastic photos?" – "I took them ________________ ."
3. "Will you help us with our homework?" – "Well, OK. But you should really do it ________________ ."
4. "Can we help Michael with his problems?" – "No, he must solve them ________________ ."
5. "I'm going to paint your room tomorrow." – "No, please don't. We want to do it ________________ ."
6. "Could you ask Danny about his plans?" – "Don't be shy, Caroline. Ask him ________________ ."
7. "Why are you angry with the girls?" – "I have to tidy their room. They never do it ________________ ."

17 A crossword

ACROSS	DOWN
4 What's the … between a mountain and a hill? 8 The boys said, "We'll help, if you like." They always … to help. 9 Jenny went to open the door when she heard the … 13 What's "wahrscheinlich" in English? Can you … it? 16 You can't see the stage until the … goes up. 18 Jess asked for help with her work because she couldn't … it alone. 20 It's hot in here. Do you … if I open the windows? 21 When you practise a play, you … 22 the clothes which an actor wears in a play	1 the opposite of "easy" 2 Paul has got lots of friends, but Fiona hasn't. She's very … of him. 3 He's an actor and she's an … 5 Tessa is the new team captain. – It's … 6 not happy 7 Nobody knows about Jack's plan. It's his … plan. 10 You keep your money in it. 11 How much money does Bob … as an actor? 12 When you clap at the end of a play, you … 14 Karen loves animals, … dogs. 15 Everybody likes Matt. He's a really cool … 17 another word for "a tip" 19 all the people who watch a play

Unit 4 The UK on the move

→ pages 58/59

What do you remember?		
Nordengland war früher eine **Gegend** mit viel **Schwerindustrie**.	The north of England was once a region with a lot of heavy industry.	☐
Vor 80 Jahren gab es viele **Kohlengruben**, aber nicht viele **bestehen** heute.	80 years ago there were many coal mines, but not many exist today.	☐
Einige Städte haben eine **Verschönerung** erfahren.	Some towns in the area have had a face lift.	☐
Die **Landschaft** ist jetzt wieder grün, und es gibt **weniger** Rauch in der Luft.	The landscape is now green again and there is less smoke in the air.	☐
Was für ein **Kontrast** zu früher!	What a contrast to earlier times!	☐
In einer Stadt ist **neulich** ein Museum eröffnet worden, in dem man **regionale** Kunst sehen kann.	A new museum has opened in one town recently which shows regional art.	☐
Im Durchschnitt besuchen es 2.000 Menschen pro Monat.	On average, 2,000 people visit it every month.	☐
Die Stadt ist sehr **stolz** darauf.	The city is very proud of it.	☐

1 Make new words or phrases

Put two halves together to make a new word or phrase.

mine face industry birth land old- high-tech fashioned lift scape place coal

1. coal mine
2. face lift
3. landscape
4. old-fashioned
5. birthplace
6. industry high-tech

2 What's missing?

Find the missing letters and finish the sentences.

1. Tina has recently found a really cool sports club. RCNTLY
2. She does sports five times a week on average. VRG
3. In her region most young people do sports at school. RGN
4. They're very proud of their school teams. PRD

→ pages 58/59

What do you remember?		
Cat besucht gern neue Orte. Sie ist immer **unterwegs**.	Cat likes to see new places. She's always on the move.	☐
Letztes Jahr nahm sie an einem **Austausch** nach Cardiff teil.	Last year she went on an exchange to Cardiff.	☐
Sie wohnte bei einer **walisischen** Familie.	She stayed with a welsh family.	☐
Nun möchte sie vielleicht nach Wales **umziehen**.	Now she thinks she'd like to move (house) to Wales.	☐
Cardiff ist der **Geburtsort** vieler berühmter Sänger.	Cardiff is the birthplace of many famous singers.	☐
Musik ist ein wichtiger Teil walisischer **Kultur**.	Music is an important part of Welsh culture.	☐
Cardiff ist auch die **Kult**hauptstadt von Rugby.	Cardiff is also the cult capital of rugby.	☐
Cats Freund spielt Rugby. Er spielt auf dem linken **Flügel**.	Cat's boyfriend plays rugby. His position is left wing.	☐
Er ist außerdem Mitglied in einem **Männerchor**.	He also belongs to a male voice choir.	☐

3 A pairs puzzle

Think about the first pair of words. Then complete the second pair.

1. players • team | singers • choir
2. England • English | Wales • welsh
3. older • younger | more • less
4. person • arms | bird • wings
5. centre • central | region • regional
6. soon • future | recently • past

4 Missing words

Find the right prepositions.

1. Most people are proud of their home town.
2. Oxford is famous for its old buildings.
3. The town has more visitors on average than Cardiff.
4. Can you find Oxford on this map?
5. There's a list of names at the back of the book.
6. What's special about Oxford High Street?

→ pages 60/61

What do you remember?		
„Kultur“ und „Liebe“ sind **abstrakte** Nomen.	“Culture” and “love” are *abstract* nouns.	☐
Es gibt zwei Arten von **Artikeln**.	There are two types of *articles* .	☐
Im Englischen ist der **bestimmte Artikel** „the“.	In English the *definite article* is “the”.	☐
Der **unbestimmte** Artikel ist entweder „a“ oder „an“.	The *indefinite* article is “a” or “an”.	☐
Tom **ist an** Kunst **interessiert** und er ist **zweisprachig**.	Tom *is interessting in* art, and he’s *bilingual* .	☐
Einige seiner **Verwandten** sind Deutsche.	Some of his *relatives* are German.	☐
Sein Vater ist **Ingenieur** bei einer großen **Firma**.	His father is an *engineer* with a big *firm* .	☐
Tom **würde lieber den Armen** helfen.	Tom *would rather* help *the poor* .	☐
Es ist **furchtbar**, wenn man sich noch nicht einmal ein neues **Paar** Schuhe kaufen kann.	It’s *awful* when people can’t even buy a new *pair of* shoes.	☐
Tom isst oft **zu Abend** bei Rajiv, weil Rajivs **Freundschaft** ihm wichtig ist.	Tom often has ___ with Rajiv because Rajiv’s *friendship* is important to him.	☐
Er mag den **Geschmack** seines leckeren Essens.	He likes the *taste* of his tasty food.	☐

5 Abstract nouns

Fill in the missing words.

home | the home | love | the love | music | the music

1 Charlotte’s favourite hobby is ___, but she’s interested in animals, too.

2 She and her friend Emma went to ___ for sick animals yesterday.

3 They know that ___ is very important for animals, too.

4 When they got back, nobody was at ___ – only Charlotte’s dog.

5 “I think ___ that dog has for you is amazing,” Emma said.

6 “Yes,” said Charlotte, “but he doesn’t always like ___ I play!”

→ page 62

What do you remember?		
Es ist nicht immer einfach, **Schwierigkeiten zu bewältigen** und **sich zu entschuldigen**.	Dealing with problems and apologizing isn't always easy.	☐
Lynn **befasst sich** selbst mit ihren Problemen.	Lynn always ______ her problems herself.	☐
Anderen **zu helfen** dauert oft nur einige Minuten.	Helping others often takes only a few minutes.	☐
Es ist wichtig, **sich zu entschuldigen**.	It's important to apologizing.	☐
Sag', „**Ich wollte** dich **nicht** verletzen."	You say, "I didn't mean to hurt you."	☐
Die höfliche Antwort ist: „**Mach dir nichts draus!**"	The polite answer is: "Never mind!"	☐
Es ist **unhöflich**, „Beeil' dich!" zu schreien.	It's rude to shout "Hurry up!"	☐
Man sagt „**Lass dir Zeit.**"	Say, "Take your time."	☐

6 Helping and apologizing

What are the people saying? Write down their words in the pictures.

1 Never mind.
2 Be more careful next time.
3 I apologize.
4 Sorry I'm so slow.
5 That's OK. Just take your time.
6 That's very kind of you.
7 Your foot! – I'm terribly sorry!
8 Can I help you?

7 Meeting new people

What can you say to somebody to start a conversation? Write down five more things.

"I'm sure we've met somewhere before."

______

______

→ pages 63–65

What do you remember?		
Die Sandhars sind eine **asiatische** Familie, die **im Norden** wohnen.	The Sandhars are an _asian_ family who live _up North_.	☐
Alle sprechen Englisch und **Pandschabi**.	They all speak English and _panshabi_.	☐
Aseems Mutter kocht **Curry**, weil es gut **schmeckt**.	Aseem's mother makes _curry_ because it _tastes_ good.	☐
Wenn die Kinder fragen, „Was **riecht** so gut?" heißt ihre **Antwort** „Wartet ab!"	When the kids ask, "What _smells_ so good?" her _reply_ is "Wait and see!"	☐
Aseem wollte gestern **Bhangra** hören, dann aber erzählte ihm Ken von einer **Ausstellung**.	Yesterday Aseem wanted to listen to _Bhangra_, but then Ken told him about an art _exhibition_.	☐
„Das **klingt** nicht sehr interessant," sagte Aseem.	"That doesn't _sounds_ very interesting," Aseem said.	☐
„Wir könnten uns auch einen **Audio**führer besorgen," sagte Ken, „und wir werden **spätestens bis** acht wieder hier sein."	"We could also get an _audio_ guide," Ken said, "and we'll be back here again _until_ eight."	☐
Tatsächlich **schien** Aseem Spaß zu haben.	In fact, Aseem _seem_ to enjoy himself.	☐

8 Verbs and adjectives – the odd word out

Cross out the wrong word.

to smell to taste ~~to sound~~ ~~to be~~	+ spicy	to feel	+ awful proud ~~tasty~~ sick	to seem ~~to taste~~ to sound to feel	+ worried	to look	+ calm friendly pretty ~~loud~~

9 'By' or 'until'?

Put in the right preposition.

1. Tim gets up at seven at the latest. = He gets up _by_ seven.
2. He doesn't leave the house before eight o'clock. = He always stays at home _until_ eight o'clock.
3. At 12 o'clock – or even earlier – he feels hungry. = He feels hungry ~~until~~ _by_ twelve o'clock.
4. After lessons he plays football from four to five o'clock. = He doesn't go home ~~by~~ _until_ five o'clock.

→ page 66

What do you remember?

Julia macht **Untersuchungen** für ihr Projekt.	Julia is doing research for her project.
Das **Thema** ihres Projektes ist **Freizeit**aktivitäten.	The topic of her project is leisure activities.
Sie hat schon viele **Sachtexte** gefunden, die sie **überfliegen** will.	She has already found many factual texts which she wants to skim .
Sie **konzentriert sich** auf wichtige **Stichworte**.	She concentrate on important keywords .
Als Nächstes will sie die Texte nach nützlichen Fakten **durchsuchen**.	Next she wants to scan the texts for useful facts.
Durch **Überfliegen** und **Durchsuchen** bekommt man Informationen.	Skimming and Scanning are good ways to get information.
Das Seebad Weston **muss man gesehen haben**.	The seaside town of Weston is a must-see .
Julia war **während** ihrer Ferien dort.	Julia was there at least her summer holidays.
Sie mag Aktivitäten im Wasser und **an Land**.	She likes activities in the water and on land .
Große Hotels sind für **Tagungen** sehr beliebt, wenn sie in der Nähe einer **Autobahn** liegen.	Big hotels are very popular for conferences if they are near a motorway .
Julia geht nie zum **Abendessen** in ein Hotel.	Julia never goes to a hotel for dinner .

10 Dialogues

Finish the dialogues with the correct phrases. (You don't need one of them.)

- scanning that text
- to the leisure centre
- on the motorway
- during our journey
- a must-see
- I must concentrate
- I'm doing research

1. "Why are you scanning that text ?"
   – "It's for my project. I'm doing research ."
2. "Let's go to Windsor Castle. It's a must-see ."
   – "OK. We can go there ~~to the leisure centre~~ during our journey ."
3. "Let's listen to music ~~during our journey~~ motorway ."
   – "No. I'm reading, and I must concentrate. ."

→ pages 67–69

What do you remember?	
Menschenmenge	A large crowd came to the football match.
jubeln	They had all come to cheer and have fun.
Es ist schade	It's a pity that it was so cold.
ausprobieren • **zum Spaß**	After the match some people went to a leisure centre and try out squash, just for laughs.
sich über jmd. lustig machen	They played badly, but the trainer didn't makes fun of them.
Akzent • **seltsam**	For some people the accent which is spoken in London sounds really weird.
Ortswechsel	Changing places is a good experience, even for one day.
Suchmaschine	If you want to find information, you can use a search engine.
interaktiv	It can help you to find some interactive websites.
ziemlich • **satt bekommen**	They're quite interesting, but you'll probably get tired of your computer.
rumhängen	It's more fun to hang out with friends.
mindestens • **Hafenviertel**	Many Liverpool teenagers spend at least one afternoon a week on the waterfront.

11 Find the word

Replace the marked word with a word from the unit that fits better.

1. All the people Wayne met in Swansea spoke **Welsh**. __________
2. He liked the museum because it was **beautiful**. __________
3. On his ferry trip in Liverpool Michael saw the docks and the **swimming pool**. __________
4. At the football match the crowd **waved wildly** when their team got the ball. __________
5. People made fun of Rhona's **clothes** in Reading. __________
6. Young people enjoy **checking out** with their friends in Windsor. __________

12 A word grid

Translate the words into English and find them in the grid.

N	I	J	L	H	P	A	C	Z	W	Y	E	M	P	X
E	X	H	I	B	I	T	I	O	N	J	O	O	C	Q
W	L	S	G	L	V	D	B	R	K	T	S	M	R	F
O	E	H	V	D	I	J	N	P	O	A	X	W	O	H
X	I	I	H	E	I	V	R	R	T	G	M	P	W	B
U	S	P	R	C	Q	T	W	N	A	B	I	S	D	Q
Z	U	A	L	D	L	A	N	D	S	C	A	P	E	J
I	R	K	I	C	Y	H	O	M	T	Z	Y	H	U	D
V	E	E	X	C	H	A	N	G	E	C	U	R	D	Q

Austausch
Landschaft
Ausstellung
Autobahn
Geschmack
seltsam
Freizeit
Menschenmenge

13 Singular or plural?

What is Louise going to pack?

1 ______________________________
2 ______________________________
3 ______________________________
4 ______________________________
5 ______________________________
6 ______________________________

14 Adjectives from nouns

-ous
-y
-al
-ful

What adjective can you make from the marked noun? Use it to finish the second sentence.

1. Who's making all that **noise**? It's not usually so noisy here.
2. Ben Nevis is the highest **mountain** in the UK. It's in a mountainous region.
3. Does Mike paint with lots of different **colours**? – Yes, he paints very colourful pictures.
4. Have you heard about Amy's latest **adventure**? – No, but I know she's a very adventurous person.
5. **Music** is very important to Frank. He can play at least four musical instruments.
6. You should be more interested in your **health**. You don't eat very healthy food.
7. Where does the **power** for your new invention come from? – I use a powerful steam engine.
8. Oh no, look at all those black **clouds**! – Don't worry. It won't stay cloudy for long.

15 A crossword

Fill in the crossword with words you learned in Unit 4.

ACROSS	DOWN
3. When you say "Sorry", you …	1. Your uncles, cousins and grandparents are your …
4. the place where somebody was born	2. He lives in London, but he wants to … to Bristol.
7. David doesn't enjoy swimming. He'd … go skateboarding.	5. not long ago
9. Please be friendly to new classmates. Don't make … of them.	6. My sister has won a prize. I'm very … of her.
10. Ed isn't rich. He's got … money than his friends.	8. another word for "terrible"
13. an important word in a text	11. Maybe I … calm, but I feel very nervous.
16. You can't come to the concert? That's a …	12. If you can speak two languages perfectly, you are …
19. a lot of people	14. another word for "strange"
21. another word for "free time"	15. the big meal you eat in the evening
22. Curry smells nice, but I don't like the …	17. Johannes speaks English with a strong German …
23. A bird uses its … to fly.	18. You mustn't use your mobile … lessons.
	20. the opposite of "polite"

Revision Unit 3 + 4

1 Odd word out

Cross out the wrong word. What links the other three words? Write down one word.

1. proud | difficult | grumpy | jealous ______
2. purse | change | leisure | to earn ______
3. cast | engineer | crowd | audience ______
4. to seem | to apologize | to chat | to translate ______
5. rehearsal | research | to perform | curtain ______

2 What's the phrase?

Find the right German phrase and complete the sentences in English.

Das ist schade. | … macht mich verrückt. | Ich wollte nicht unhöflich sein. | … macht sich über mich lustig. | Das ist mir egal. | Da ist was dran.

1. "John can't come to the party." – "______ . He's so nice."
2. "If you don't come, you'll hurt Paul's feelings." – "______ .
   I hadn't thought about it like that."
3. "My mother tells me to tidy my room five times a day. She ______ !"
4. "Oh, sorry! Were you talking to someone else? ______ ."
5. "Hey, you're sitting on my DVDs!"– "______ ! I'm not getting up!"
6. "Why don't you like my brother?" – "He ______ ."

3 How much do you remember?

Write down words you know from Unit 3 and Unit 4 under these headings.

culture	at home	getting on with people

Unit 5 Media messages

→ pages 76/77

What do you remember?		
Ich wäre gerne eine **berühmte Persönlichkeit** wie Lady Gaga.	I wish I were a ______ like Lady Gaga.	☐
Die **Medien** lieben sie und sie ist immer in den **Boulevardzeitungen**.	The ______ love her and she's always in the ______ .	☐
	Even the ______ ______ sometimes have articles about her, too.	☐
Ihre Fans **machen** sie gern **nach**.	Her fans love to ______ her.	☐
Sie liebt es, in ihrem **Studio** neue Lieder zu schreiben.	She loves to write new songs in her ______ .	☐
Sie tritt auch gern in der **Öffentlichkeit** auf.	She loves to perform in ______, too.	☐
Ihr letztes **Konzert** war toll.	Her last ______ was great.	☐
Die Atmosphäre, die sie auf der Bühne **geschaffen hat**, war **spitze**.	The atmosphere she ______ on stage was ______ .	☐
Ihr Album „Born This Way" hat über eine Million **Exemplare** in der ersten Woche verkaufte.	Her album "Born This Way" sold more than one million ______ in the first week.	☐

1 Odd one out

Underline the word that doesn't fit in.

1. favourite • awesome • violence • realistic
2. single • record • album • concert
3. tips • news • advice • information
4. click • Internet • download • send
5. product • TV • newspaper • radio
6. reporter • actor • teenager • DJ

2 Sounds: One sound makes a difference

Find the right word.

1	The simple past of 'to make':		Another word for a friend:	
2	You carry things in this:		The opposite of 'front':	
3	It's at the end of your leg:		What we all eat:	

→ pages 76/77

What do you remember?	
Fernseh**sendungen** sind eine beliebte Form von **Unterhaltung** für die Briten.	TV ______ are a popular form of ______ for the British.
Vor allem lieben sie ihre **Seifenopern**.	They especially love their ______ .
Sie **machen** keine **Werbung** für **Seife** oder für andere **Reinigungsmittel**, die die **Hausfrauen** kaufen sollten.	They don't ______ ______ or other ______ ______ should buy.
Sie versuchen, das Leben so **realistisch** wie möglich zu präsentieren.	They try to be as ______ about life as possible.
Die Geschichten **verändern sich**.	The stories ______ .
Aber die **Haupt**themen – Liebe, Probleme und etwas **Gewalt** – bleiben gleich.	But the ______ themes – love, problems and some ______ – remain the same.
Die Seifenoper Coronation Street, die den **Spitznamen** „Corrie" hat, startete 1960.	Coronation Street, which has the ______ "Corrie", began in 1960.

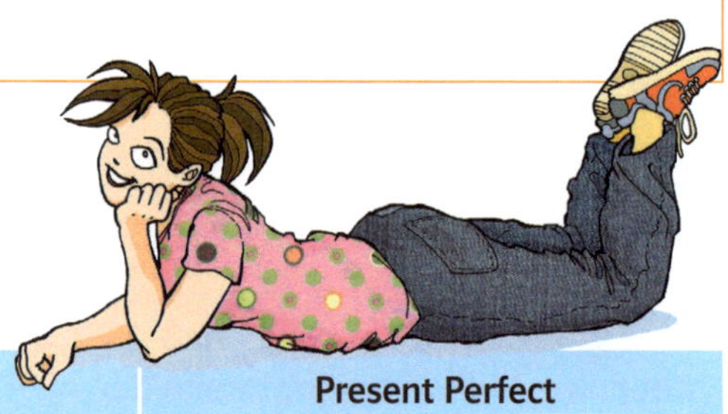

3 Irregular verbs

Complete the grid with the right verb forms.

	Infinitive	Simple Past	Present Perfect
1.	to break		have/has broken
2.	to show	showed	
3.	to write		have/has written
4.	to choose	chose	
5.	to teach		
6.	to give		have/has given
7.	to take	took	
8.	to tell		
9.	to bring		
10.	to catch		
11.	to grow		have/has grown
12.	to think		
13.	to steal		

→ pages 78–80

What do you remember?		
Vor zwei Wochen rief mich mein **Agent** an.	Two weeks ago my ______ called me.	☐
Er hatte ein **Drehbuch** für einen neuen Film und wollte die Rolle von ‚Jake' mit mir **besprechen**.	He had a ______ for a new film and wanted to ______ the role of 'Jake' with me.	☐
Vor sechs Monaten hatte er mich  und die Fotos in seine **Akte** gesteckt.	Six months ago he had ______ me and put the photos into his ______ .	☐
Nun rief mich sein **Assistent** an und sagte: „Wir wollen eine Szene mit dir **drehen**!"	Now his ______ called me and said, "We want to ______ a scene with you!"	☐

4 False friends

a) *Translate the German words into English to complete the sentences.*

1. Tom is going to ______ a new bike for his birthday. **bekommen**
2. You don't have to write full sentences. Just make ______ . **Notizen**
3. I like your ______ . Where did you buy it? **Rock**
4. The two boys like the same ______ of music. **Art**
5. Mum ______ go shopping this afternoon. **will**
6. You ______ pick me up from the station. I can walk. **musst nicht**
7. Let's walk around the ______ in the park. **See**

b) *Translate the marked words into German.*

1. I'm not sure where Bristol is. Have you got a **map**? ______
2. If you don't know the **meaning** of a word, look it up in the dictionary. ______
3. I didn't enjoy the play. There wasn't much **action**. ______
4. Are you travelling to London by train or by **coach**? ______
5. Tom would like to buy some new **trainers** but he doesn't want ______
   to **spend** more than £20. ______

→ pages 78–80

What do you remember?		
Er schickte mir zum Lernen des Texts das **Skript** zu.	He sent me the ______________ to rehearse the text.	☐
Ich las es einmal und dann **las** ich es **noch einmal** – mindestens fünfmal.	I read them once and then I ______________ them – at least five times.	☐
Ich war mir sicher, dass der Regisseur mir **die Rolle** als Jake **geben** würde.	I was sure that the director would ______________ me as Jake.	☐
Die Rolle war **super** für mich.	The role was ______________ for me.	☐
„**Mach dir nicht zu viele Hoffnungen**", sagte meine Mutter.	"______________", my mother said.	☐
Aber ich wollte **entdeckt** werden und ich hatte Glück.	But I wanted to be ______________ and I was lucky.	☐
Mir wurde ein **Vertrag von** dem Studio angeboten.	I was offered a ______________ ______________ the studio.	☐
Heute werde ich ihn **unterschreiben**.	Today I'm going to ______________ it.	☐

5 Wordsearch

Translate the words and find them in the grid.

Drehbuch · Sendung · Handy · Seifenoper · Zeitschrift · Zeitung · Nachrichten · Schauspieler · Werbung machen · Werbespot

N	N	E	W	S	P	A	P	E	R	O	T	C	A	R
E	D	V	C	O	M	M	E	R	C	I	A	L	N	P
W	I	Y	M	A	G	A	Z	I	N	E	H	C	W	L
S	C	R	I	P	T	A	D	V	E	R	T	I	S	E
L	M	O	B	I	L	E	M	M	A	R	G	O	R	P

6 Find the missing word

Look at the first pair of words and find the missing word.

1. early • late | active • ______________
2. music • to listen | TV • ______________
3. to copy • copied | to cast • ______________
4. to inform • information | to live • ______________
5. celeb • celebrity | fave • ______________
6. men • women | actors • ______________

→ page 81

What do you remember?		
Verbringst du viel Zeit vor dem Fernseher? Bist du eine  ?	Do you spend a lot of time in front of the TV? Are you a ______________________ ?	☐
Oder liebst du Bücher? Bist du ein **Bücherwurm**?	Or do you love books? Are you a ______________________ ?	☐
Vielleicht liebst du auch Musik und bist ein Musik**verrückter**.	Or maybe you're crazy about music and you're a music ______________________ .	☐
Heute **diskutieren** wir über das **Pro und Kontra** der Medien.	Today we're ______________________ the ______________________ of the media.	☐

7 What's in an ad?

Translate the words in the box and complete the text.

The picture shows a pretty girl with dark brown curly ______________ Haare and ______________ große dark brown ______________ Augen . She ______________ trägt a ______________ weißes football shirt and ______________ schwarze shorts. She ______________ steht in front of the goal.

The fans ______________ jubeln wildly and she ______________ lächelt happily because she ______________ hat gerade geschossen the winning goal.

The ______________ Anzeige is for toothpaste. When you look at the ______________ Bild , it gives you the ______________ Gefühl that if you use this toothpaste, you'll have a ______________ wunderhübsches smile and you'll be a ______________ Gewinner , too.

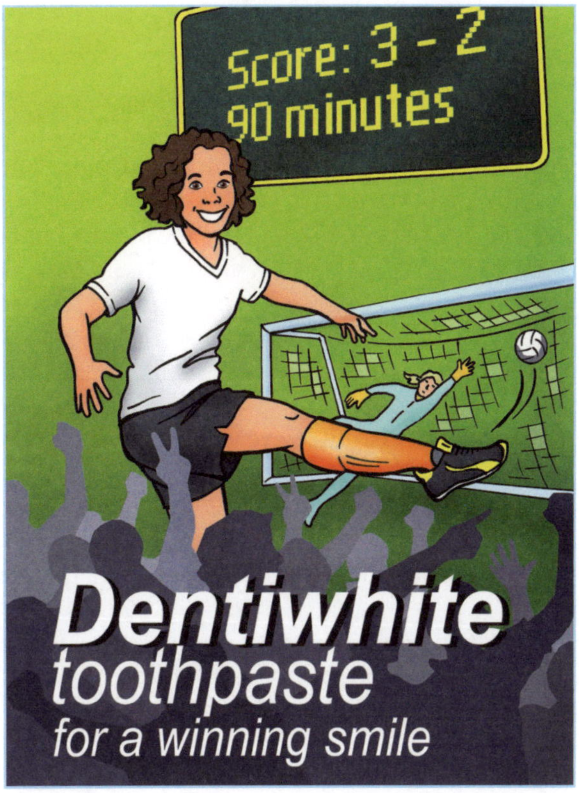

→ pages 82–84

What do you remember?	
Jedes Jahr wird viel Geld für **Werbung** ausgegeben.	Every year a lot of money is spent on ________________.
Gute **Werbespots** sind teuer.	Good ________________ are expensive.
Aber sie **sind** es immer **wert**, auch wenn das **Produkt**, das du kaufen willst, nur  ist.	But they ________________ always ________________ it, even if the ________________ you are trying to sell is only a small ________________ of hair gel.
Um **auf sich aufmerksam** zu **machen**, braucht man eine gute **Schlagzeile**.	To ________________ people's ________________ you need a good ________________.
Eine berühmte Persönlichkeit wie ein bekannter **Fußball**spieler kann auch hilfreich sein.	A celeb like a famous ________________ player can be very helpful, too.
Oder man zeigt einen Menschen mit einem besonderen **Aussehen**, z. B. eine hübsche Frau mit glänzenden, **glatten** Haaren.	Or you show a person with a special ________________, e.g. a beautiful woman with shiny, ________________ hair.

8 Useful phrases: How to check each other's ad

Choose the right phrases to complete the dialogue.

I think I'll do that. | Thanks. | If I were you, I would … | I know what you mean. | I'll change that | that's a good idea. | It would be better if you …

Pupil A: Could you have a look at my ad and tell me what you think of it, please?

Pupil B: Yes, of course. Hm. I like the picture but I'm not so sure about the text. ________________ try to make it a little more exciting.

Pupil A: Yes, ________________. It *is* a bit boring, isn't it? Have you got any ideas how to improve it?

Pupil B: ________________ used a few more positive adjectives. You know, like 'awesome' or 'cool'.

Pupil A: Oh, ________________. Yes, ________________.

Pupil B: I also think you need a better headline. You know, one that will get the reader's attention.

Pupil A: Yes, you're right. ________________, too. ________________.

→ page 85

What do you remember?	
Neulich **organisierte** unsere Jugendgruppe eine **LAN** Party, um **Geld zu sammeln**.	Recently our youth group ______ an ______ party to ______.
Sie wurde von ca. 70 Teenagern **besucht**.	It was ______ by about 70 teenagers.
Die Organisatoren hatten versprochen, im **Hintergrund** zu bleiben, wenn wir versprechen würden, ein paar **Grund**regeln zu befolgen:	The organisers had promised to stay in the ______ if we promised to follow a few ______ rules:
	No alcohol was ______.
Und wir durften nicht zu viel **Lärm** machen.	And we weren't allowed to make too much ______.
Wir **äußerten** alle unsere **Meinung** zu diesen Regeln, und einige wurden **neu geschrieben**.	We all ______ our ______ on these rules, some of them were ______.
Am **Anfang** war alles echt witzig.	At the ______ everything was great.
Ich habe viele neue Leute kennengelernt und wir **haben** Telefonnummern **ausgetauscht**.	I met lots of new people and we ______ phone numbers.
Aber dann ist ein **Streit** ausgebrochen.	But then an ______ broke out.
Ein paar Teenager, die **gewalttätig** wurden, mussten von ihren Eltern von der **Polizeidienststelle** abgeholt werden.	A few teenagers who became ______ had to be picked up by their parents at the ______.

9 Verb friends

Match these nouns with the right verb.

an exercise, glasses, a party, the shopping, lunch, a noise, homework, a concert, information, addresses, trousers, ideas, a helmet, a school, a mistake

exchange	make	do	wear	attend

→ pages 86/87

What do you remember?	
	Bill never reads anything, not even the ______________________ box.
jmdn. zu etwas bewegen	Nobody can ______________________ to read a book.
überzeugen	Nobody can ______________________ him.
Magie	But then one day his mother brought him a book about ______________ .
Stapel • herunterfallen • verschwinden	Bill put it next to the ______________________ of books which often ______________________ his desk. Then the book just ______________________ behind his bed, somehow.
Rampe	There it stayed until he needed it for his skateboard ______________ .
(zer)brechen	At first Bill had great fun but then his skateboard ______________________ in two and Bill broke his leg.
Erkältung • Spinat	While he was in hospital, he got a ______________________ , and he had to eat ______________________ every day.
zugeben	But then he finally started to read the Harry Potter book and had to ______________________ that it was really good.

10 Spot the mistake

In each sentence there is one mistake. Underline it and write down the correct word on the line.

1. The girl in the ad had beautiful shiny hairs. ______________________
2. Bill was examined from a doctor. ______________________
3. My agent gave me a good advice. ______________________
4. After the fight broke out, the police was called. ______________________
5. The girls are going to drive to London by train. ______________________
6. The cartoon show two people: a woman and her son. ______________________
7. What is your meaning of the magazine? ______________________
8. Many small children doesn't like spinach. ______________________

→ pages 86/87

What do you remember?		
vorbeigehen • oben	Janice ______ an old metal factory when she hears a strange noise from ______ .	☐
 • Umriss	On the ______ she sees the ______ of a small boy.	☐
tiefe Schnittwunde	He is crying because he has a big ______ on his leg.	☐
sich schneiden	He ______ himself on a piece of metal.	☐
Rohr	Janice sees a ______ and climbs up.	☐
Blut	There is ______ everywhere.	☐
Notfall	It's an ______ .	☐
binden • Patient • ablenken	She ______ her T-shirt around his leg and tells her ______ a joke to ______ him.	☐
Verband • fest • 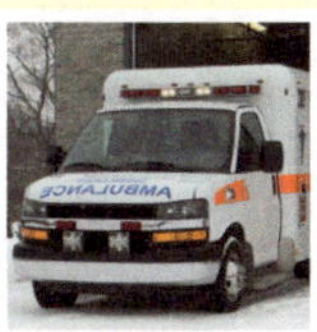	As soon as the ______ is ______ , she calls an ______ .	☐
wird gerettet	And the boy ______ .	☐

11 Pronunciation

Match these words with the right sound.

country · plate · ground · basic · enough ✓ · trouble · blood · raise · shout · allow ✓ · trousers · great ✓

ʌ	enough			
au	allow			
ei	great			

12 Word families

Find the nouns of the following verbs.

1. to advertise ______
2. to bleed ______
3. to smell ______
4. to feel ______
5. to invite ______
6. to fly ______

13 Be more polite

Look at the following situations. Some people in the pictures aren't very polite. Try to make the conversations more polite.

1

____

____

____

____

2

____

____

____

____

3

____

____

____

____

14 A mind map: Media

Complete the mind map with words you learned in Unit 5. You can also add other words you know.

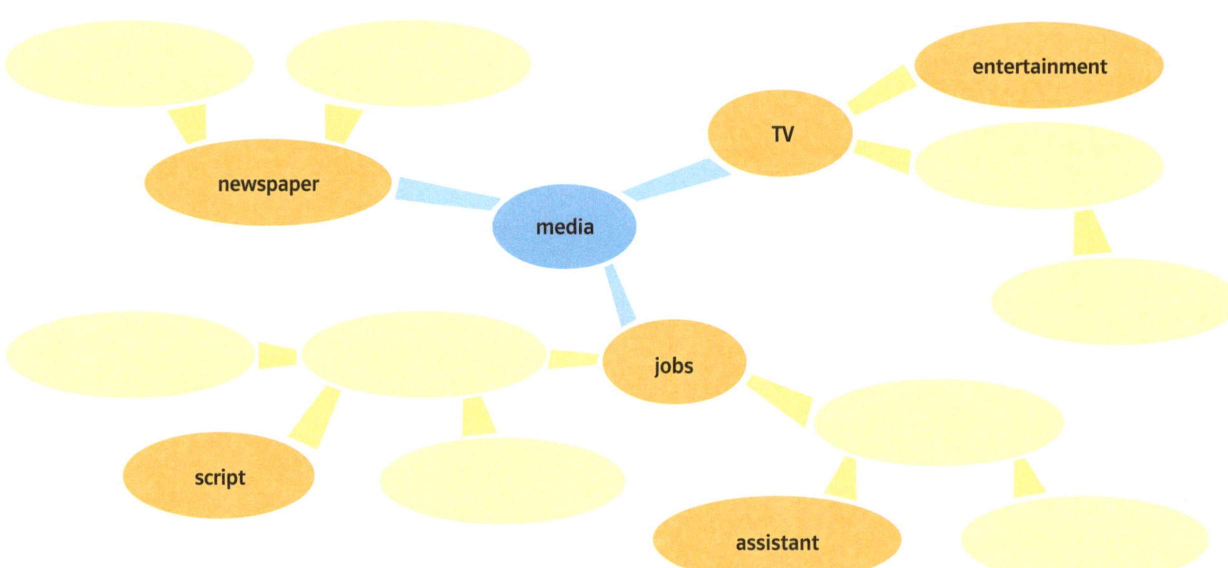

15 A crossword

ACROSS

1. the plural of 'housewife'
5. a green vegetable
7. The letter was … by a man called John Ben.
10. a kind of folder you keep papers in
11. tooth • teeth; medium • …
13. a famous film star, actor or model
14. feet • foot; copies • …
15. What … of music do you like?
17. the written text of a play or film
18. another word for 'great'
19. 'The Beeb' is a … for the BBC.
21. Did Amy … Jack to her party?
23. Please be quiet. You're making too much …
24. Only make a 999 call in an …
26. Your hair looks a mess. Please … it back.

DOWN

2. Let's sing the … in English.
3. the English word for 'Unterhaltung'
4. different • difference; violent • …
6. another word for a TV advertisement
7. you wash your hands with this
8. The Sun is a popular …
9. It's only a small cut. You don't need a …
12. the opposite of 'ending'
16. the English word for 'glatt'
18. the opposite of 'passive'
20. That T-shirt is too … You need a larger size.
22. the opposite of 'south'
25. bike • ride; … • drive

Unit 6 Time to travel

→ pages 92/93

What do you remember?	
Wie viel weißt du über berühmte **Reisende**?	How much do you know about famous ___________?
Wer schrieb ein Buch über die **Evolution**?	Who wrote a book about ___________?
Was hat Marco Polo von China nach Europa mitgebracht? **Nudeln** oder die Kartoffel**pflanze**?	What did Marco Polo bring back to Europe from China? ___________ or the potato ___________?
Wie lange **dauerte** seine **Reise** durch Asien?	How long did his ___________ through Asia ___________?
Welche britische **Missionärin** hat Kindern in China geholfen?	Which British ___________ helped children in China?
Wer sagte: „Das ist ein kleiner **Schritt** für einen Menschen, aber ein **Riesensprung** für die **Menschheit**", als er 1969 auf dem landete?	Who said: "That's one small ___________ for a man, but one ___________ for ___________" when he landed on the ___________ in 1969?
Was war Ellen MacArthurs größte **Herausforderung**?	What was Ellen MacArthur's greatest ___________?
Warum ist Englisch die **Muttersprache** von mehr als 330 Millionen Menschen?	Why is English the ___________ of more than 330 million people?
Warum werden 85 **Prozent** aller Nachrichten im Internet in Englisch verschickt?	Why are 85 ___________ of all Internet messages sent in English?

1 Word puzzle

Find nine words to do with air travel.

val cus ture port bag sen par de port ket air
ri off ger ar tic toms take pas pass gage

1. ___________ 4. ___________ 7. ___________

2. ___________ 5. ___________ 8. ___________

3. ___________ 6. ___________ 9. ___________

→ pages 94/95

What do you remember?		
Die indirekte Rede benutzt du, wenn du **wiedergeben** willst, was ein anderer gesagt hat.	You use indirect speech when you want to ______ what somebody has said.	☐
Um die indirekte Rede **einzuleiten**, brauchst du ein besonderes Verb wie *sagen* oder *erzählen*.	To ______ indirect speech you need a special verb like *to say* or *to tell*.	☐
Tim **erwähnte**, dass er **am Tag zuvor** von seinem Urlaub in England zurückgekehrt sei.	Tim ______ that he had got back from his holiday in England ______ .	☐
Das Wetter sei **enttäuschend** gewesen und der Regen habe erst **zwei Tage zuvor** aufgehört.	The weather had been ______ and the rain had only stopped ______ .	☐
	But he said that his host family had given him a warm ______ and they had been very friendly.	☐
Er **habe sich** manchmal ein bisschen **gelangweilt**.	Sometimes he ______ a bit ______ .	☐

2 Indirect speech with reporting verb in the past

Complete the grids.

Direct speech		Indirect speech
is	→	
are going	→	
think	→	
writes	→	
can	→	
must	→	
may	→	

Direct speech		Indirect speech
was/were	→	
saw	→	
enjoyed	→	
had	→	
have/has done	→	
had visited	→	
will know	→	

Direct speech		Indirect speech
here	→	
this	→	
come	→	
bring	→	
yesterday	→	

Direct speech		Indirect speech
today	→	
tomorrow	→	
last week	→	
next year	→	
two days ago	→	

→ page 96

What do you remember?		
Kannst du mir einen **Rat** geben?	Can you give me some ______________________ ?	☐
Kannst du ein guten Film **empfehlen**?	Can you ______________________ a good film?	☐
Wie wäre es mit einer **Komödie**, z. B. „Knight and Day"?	How about a ______________________, 'Knight and Day', for example?	☐
Wer spielt mit?	______________________ ?	☐
Tom Cruise. Hast du seine **Biografie** schon gelesen? Sie ist sehr interessant.	Tom Cruise. Have you read his ______________________ ? It's very interesting.	☐

3 Questions with prepositions

Fill in the missing prepositions.

1. Who took this photo ____________ you?
2. What does Sue usually spend her pocket money ____________ ?
3. Why isn't Ben talking ____________ David? Have they had an argument?
4. What were you laughing ____________ ?
5. What kind of films are you interested ____________ ?
6. What kind of problems do the police have to deal ____________ ?

4 Talking about a film

Put these sentences into the right order.

1. It's a thriller. I can really recommend it.	☐
2. Oh yes. It's one of the most exciting films I've ever seen.	☐
3. If I tell you that, it might spoil[1] it for you.	☐
4. Have you seen Daniel Radcliffe's new film 'The Woman in Black'?	☐
5. Well, you can at least tell me if it's exciting.	☐
6. Cool, I like thrillers. What's it about?	☐
7. No, not yet. What kind of film is it?	☐
8. Can you recommend any good films?	☐

[1] **spoil** verderben

→ pages 97–99

What do you remember?		
Gestern gab es einen schweren Unfall mit einem LKW und einem **Reisebus**.	Yesterday there was a bad accident between a lorry and a ______________ .	☐
Der LKW war mit **gefährlichen Chemikalien** beladen.	The lorry was carrying ______________ .	☐
Der LKW-Fahrer hat alle **gewarnt**, schnell wegzurennen.	The driver ______________ everybody to run away fast.	☐
Zum Glück war niemand **eingeklemmt**.	Luckily nobody was ______________ .	☐
Ich habe den Not**dienst** gerufen.	I called the emergency ______________ .	☐
Feuerwehrmänner, Sanitäter und die Polizei kamen alle schnell an.	______________ , ______________ and the police all arrived quickly.	☐
Die **Polizeibeamten** haben mich gefragt, **ob** ich den Unfall gesehen hätte.	The ______________ asked me ______________ I had seen the accident.	☐
Dann **haben** sie mich **gebeten**, wieder in mein Auto einzusteigen und schnell wegzufahren.	Then they ______________ me to get back into my car and to leave quickly.	☐
Sie **haben** allen Autofahrern **geraten**, das **Gebiet** so schnell wie möglich zu verlassen.	They ______________ all drivers to leave the ______________ as quickly as possible.	☐

5 An emergency call

Complete Jack's emergency call to the police.

burglar · officers · help · calm · noise · name · address · on my own · I'm calling

Police officer: Dorchester Police. How can I ______________ you?

Jack: ______________ from 29, London Road. Please come quickly. I think there's a ______________ in my house. I can hear a strange ______________ downstairs.

Police officer: OK. So your ______________ is 29, London Road. And what's your ______________ ?

Jack: It's Jack Benson. Please hurry. My parents are out and I'm here ______________ .

Police officer: OK, Jack. Don't worry. Just try to keep ______________ . Two police ______________ are already on their way.

→ page 100

What do you remember?	
Sie warten auch auf den Flug nach Frankfurt, **nicht wahr**? Er wird leider Verspätung haben. – Oh, das ist **ärgerlich**.	You're waiting for the flight to Frankfurt, too, ______________ ? I think it's going to be late. – Oh, that's ______________ .
Ihr Deutsch ist **fantastisch**. – Danke. Deutsch ist meine **Zweitsprache**. Meine Mutter ist Berlinerin.	Your German is ______________ . – Thanks. German is my ______________ . My mother is from Berlin.
Was bedeutet ‚Well'? – Eigentlich nichts. Es ist ein **zusätzliches** Wort, das Leute manchmal verwenden, wenn sie sprechen. Es ist nur ein **Füllwort**.	What does 'Well' mean? – Nothing really. It's an ______________ word that people sometimes use when they're speaking. It's only a ______________ .
Es war schön dich wiederzusehen. – **Gleichfalls**. Pass auf dich auf und komm gut nach Hause.	It was nice to see you again. – ______________ . Take care and have a good journey home.

6 Jumbled sentences

Make sentences.

1. you • for • the • too? • Are • Plymouth • waiting • train • to

____

2. Yes, • am. • I • it's • running • I'm afraid • late. • fifteen minutes

____

3. that • Oh dear, • annoying. • is • I • be • ferry port • at • have to • 10.30. • by • the

____

4. Oh no! • you • Are • somewhere • going • nice?

____

5. I'm • to • going • Yes, • Rennes.

____

6. Oh • really? • there • I've • a few times. • been • It's • beautiful • a • place.

____

____

7. sure • have • time • great • there. • I'm • you'll • a

____

→ pages 101–103

What do you remember?		
Wette	Phileas Fogg has made a ____________ that he can travel around the world in eighty days.	☐
Eisenbahn	In this part of the story he is travelling from San Francisco to New York by ____________ .	☐
Sitzplatz	His manservant Passepartout and Aouda are in the two ____________ next to him.	☐
Prinzessin • retten	Aouda is a beautiful ____________ whose life they ____________ while they were in India.	☐
beenden	Fogg must ____________ his journey by 21st December.	☐
Verspätung	It's important that he gets to New York without any ____________ .	☐
schaffen • pünktlich	He has to ____________ it there ____________ .	☐
Prairie	The first problem comes while they are travelling through the ____________ of Nevada.	☐
langsamer werden	The train suddenly ____________ and stops.	☐
Gebrüll • furchterregend • sich zu Tode erschrecken	There's a loud ____________ which is so ____________ that the stewardess almost ____________ .	☐
Gleis • 	Aouda looks out of the window and on the ____________ she sees about ten thousand ____________ .	☐

7 Word search

Seven different reporting verbs for indirect speech are hidden in this box. Find them and write them down on the lines.

M	E	N	T	I	O	N	S	D	P
A	C	R	E	X	P	L	A	I	N
S	W	A	L	B	M	R	Y	O	S
K	O	W	L	A	D	V	I	S	E

____

____

____

____

→ pages 101–103

What do you remember?		
weiterfahren	After some time they are able to ______ their journey until they reach a bridge which is not safe.	☐
Haut • zu Fuß • Gefahr	A man with dark ______ has come ______ from the next station to warn them of the ______ .	☐
das Risiko eingehen	The train driver wants to ______ anyway.	☐
Pfiff • Seite	A loud ______ sounds; the train races onto the bridge and reaches the other ______ .	☐
Schrei • Sioux Indianer	But suddenly there are loud ______ as hundreds of ______ begin to attack the train.	☐
schießen •  • schreien	When they ______ into the carriages with their ______ , the passengers ______ .	☐

8 Verbs and nouns with the same form

paint · drink · work · scream

Pick the right words to complete the sentences. Decide whether you need a verb or a noun.

1. Mum, I'm thirsty. Have we got anything ______ , please?
   – Yes, there are some ______ on the kitchen table.
2. I heard a loud ______ but I've no idea who ______ or why.
3. My Dad ______ for a bank in town but he isn't at ______ today because he's ill.
4. Dad wants to ______ the living room so he has bought some yellow ______ .

9 Make verbs from nouns

Rewrite these sentences. Use verbs instead of nouns.

1. There is a beautiful **smell** from the roses.

______

2. Have you made any **plans** for this weekend?

______

3. After the game the sports star gave a reporter an **interview**.

______

10 Same sounds – different words

Fill in the correct words.

1 [weðə]	The ______ isn't very good today so I'm not sure ______ we'll be able to go swimming.
2 [ðeə]	Do you know what David and Sue are doing? – Yes, ______ talking to ______ friends over ______ .
3 [hɪə]	Mum, I'm at Ben's house. It's very loud ______ . Can you ______ me?
4 [weə]	Do you know ______ my new trousers are? I'd like to ______ them.
5 [si:]	I didn't ______ any sharks while I was swimming in the ______ .
6 [raɪt]	Do you ______ with your left or with your ______ hand?

11 Guess new words

a) *Guess the meaning of the words in the boxes from the context.*

1. This is the last **call** for passenger Andrew MacDonald. Please **proceed** to Gate 24 immediately.

______ ______

2. This is a **security announcement** . Please do not leave any bags **unattended** .

______ ______

3. May we remind you that all electronic **devices** must be **switched off** during take-off and landing.

______ ______

b) *Now guess the meaning of the words in the boxes from the word family.*

1. Tom got home very late last night. He gave me no **explanation** and made no **apology** .

______ ______

2. I got quite a **fright** when I saw the dog. It just **appeared** from nowhere.

______ ______

3. I loved Rebecca's story. It was both **imaginative** and **entertaining** .

______ ______

12 Cryptogram

In this puzzle every number stands for a letter. The same numbers mean the same letters. Try to find all of the words. There is one word to help you at the beginning. Good luck!

beginning word:

B	I	O	G	R	A	P	H	Y
11	13	3	10	18	5	6	9	20

		O		A	P			H	G	B
1	2	3	4	5	6	7	8	9	10	11

	I					R		Y		
12	13	14	15	16	17	18	19	20	21	22

1. 11 17 1 1 5 12 3
2. 5 2 2 3 20 13 2 10
3. 4 13 7 7 13 3 2 5 18 20
4. 6 18 13 2 16 15 7 7
5. 6 5 18 5 4 15 19 13 16
6. 16 9 5 12 12 15 2 10 15
7. 21 3 17 18 2 15 20
8. 1 13 18 15 1 13 10 9 14 15 18
9. 1 18 13 10 9 14 15 2 13 2 10
10. 19 13 7 5 6 6 3 13 2 14 13 2 10
11. 14 18 5 22 15 12 12 15 18
12. 11 17 18 10 12 5 18
13. 7 16 18 15 5 4
14. 5 19 22 13 16 15
15. 18 15 16 3 4 4 15 2 19
16. 8 9 15 14 9 15 18
17. 19 5 2 10 15 18 3 17 7
18. 18 5 13 12 8 5 20
19. 8 9 13 7 14 12 15
20. 16 3 2 14 13 2 17 15

Revision Unit 5 + 6

1 Word families

Which nouns go with these adjectives?

1. cloudy • cloud
2. safe • ______
3. violent • ______
4. sunny • ______
5. different • ______
6. secret • ______
7. friendly • ______
8. dangerous • ______

2 Word groups

Translate these words into English and complete the lists below.

Schauspielerin • Gepäck • Anzeige • Reisebüro • Krankenschwester • Agent • Eisenbahn • Reisepass • Zeitschrift • Sanitäter • Polizeibeamte • Flug • Drehbuch • Schlagzeile • Autobahn • Zeitungsbericht • Feuerwehrmann • Reisebus

1 jobs: ______

2 travel: ______

3 media: ______

3 Spot the mistake

In each sentence there is one mistake. Underline it and write down the correct version.

1. The operator asked me which service I need. ______
2. He said me that the police were on their way. ______
3. The bus driver warned all to get off the bus quickly. ______
4. The police officers wanted to know what was my name. ______
5. The firefighters told us to don't go near the coach. ______
6. The paramedic asked the boy if he is hurt in the accident. ______

4 Indirect speech

Complete these sentences with a fitting introductory verb. Don't use the same verb twice.

1. Yesterday Tom's agent ______ him that a casting drirector was looking for a young actor.
2. He ______ that he needed somebody with a cool look.
3. The agent ______ Tom to attend the casting.
4. But he ______ him not to get his hopes up too high.

Unit 1

What do you remember?
baseball – bat • American • field • base – base • referee – controls • pitch • rugby – oval • helmet – skateboarding • athletics – track

1 Sports
1. pitch • hands • referee • controls 2. track • run • throw
3. American • hits • bat • base • base

What do you remember?
racket • umpire – court • cricket – go on • race – brakes • ice hockey – ice – sticks

2 A crossword
1. athletics 2. track 3. umpire 4. pitch
5. skateboarding 6. baseball 7. court

Solution: cricket

What do you remember?
event • feeling – chances • won't open – until • situation • arrangements

3 Word search

A	U	N	T	I	L	R	B	S	T	Y	R	T	U	S	S	G
E	E	E	R	G	N	O	B	A	E	F	U	R	T	S	G	L
S	V	R	Y	Y	U	M	U	S	I	T	U	A	T	I	O	N
O	T	E	G	T	X	S	J	W	F	G	J	I	X	B	P	E
P	F	F	N	U	H	A	M	E	R	I	C	A	N	R	E	R
C	S	V	D	T	L	X	I	D	X	D	C	O	G	U	N	E
E	D	J	A	R	R	A	N	G	E	M	E	N	T	S	E	W

arrangements • open • event • American • until • situation

4 Spot the mistakes
1. helmet, skateboarding
2. doesn't / won't, wins
3. Baseball, American

What do you remember?
Agreeing – disagreeing • to agree • wheelchair • once • luck • exactly • rubbish

5 Agreeing and disagreeing
Lösungsvorschlag:
2. Don't be silly! Cricket can be fun and it's very popular with lots of people. / That's what I think, too. It's a boring game because there isn't very much action.
3. Rubbish! Girls can play rugby as well as boys and there are many successful women's teams. / You're right. The sport is too hard for women, they shouldn't play a men's sport.
4. I don't agree. Winning is the most important thing when you do a sport. / Exactly! Winning isn't the most important thing. You do sports to have lots of fun.
5. I don't think that's true. Referees are only people and can make mistakes, too. / I agree. Referees know the rules best and the players should listen to them.
6. Sorry, but you're wrong. It's never OK to hurt somebody, even if you're trying to win a game. / That's what I think, too. Some sports can be very physical and you sometimes hurt somebody if you're trying to win.

What do you remember?
American football – halves • commercial break • channel – which / that – commercials • unusual – scientists – athletes – lungs – rowing • gold medal – swimming – disabled • record

6 Sports and pictures
Lösungsvorschlag:
Football:
referee, grass pitch, kick, ball
Baseball:
base, bat, field
Athletics:
track, run, jump, throw
American Football:
oval ball, field, halves
Tennis:
umpire, racket, court

What do you remember?
relative clause – relative pronoun – contact clause • which / that – bobsleigh • love • whose • marathon – sweat • also • snow • oddities • exact – definition

7 Definitions
Lösungsvorschlag:
1. It comes down from the sky when it's very cold.
2. It's the highest prize you can get in a sport.
3. advertisements which are shown between TV programmes
4. the highest score or fastest time in a sport
5. It's used for races on ice.
6. In this sport you do a race in a boat.
7. It's what you do when it's very hot.
8. something unusual

What do you remember?
ski jumping – tradition – ski jumper – Eagle • press conference – van • glasses – misted up – goggles • slid – flapped – could • far – place – waved

8 An interview with Eddie
Are you sad that you didn't jump as far as the others? • It was only good enough for the last place, but I'm happy because I had the chance to go to the Olympic Games. • Did you have any problems with your glasses when you were jumping? • Yes, I did. They misted up when I put on my goggles. • Thank you for the interview and good luck for the future!

What do you remember?
context

9 What's the context?
Lösungsvorschlag:
You're welcome:
Thanks for your help – You're welcome.
pardon:
Pardon? – I said, "Could you pass me the salt, please?"
side:
There was a woman on the other side of the road.
page:
Please turn to page 38.

channel:
This show is boring. Can I switch the channel?
programme:
I like TV programmes about animals.
range:
We have a new range of bicycles in our shop.
agenda:
We should talk about the agenda for the meeting tomorrow.
to remind:
Please remind me to pack my socks.
to remember:
Was that girl at the party, too? I don't remember her.

10 Find the right words
tournament • keeper • outcome • mashed potatoes • Egyptian statues • spaceships • aliens

11 Jumbled words
baseball:
bat, field, helmet, referee, base
swimming:
water, goggles, gold medal
rugby:
oval ball, field, helmet, referee
skateboarding:
helmet, skateboard
ice-hockey:
ice, helmet, stick, referee
ski jump:
helmet, goggles, gold medal, snow
cricket:
bat, field, helmet, referee

12 Words as verbs and nouns
1. N 2. N 3. V • N 4. N • N 5. V • N 6. N • V 7. V

13 Words that you link
1. There is an unusual athlete in the competition.
2. Anne ate an apple.
3. He put on his uniform and left.
4. Almost everyone can find a sport that they like.
4. It isn't important to win.
5. I had an accident: I fell off my skateboard!

14 A crossword
Across:
1. court 4. race 5. who 8. a chair with wheels disabled people can use 10. a sport you do in the water 11. event 12. control 14. tradition 16. love 17. feelings 18. You put it on when you swim under water.

Down:
2. the person who controls a tennis match 3. snow 4. racket 6. oddity 7. definition 9. helmet 12. a sport that has a long tradition in England 13. a sport which is popular in America 15. van

Unit 2

What do you remember?
Once upon a time • heir – Norman • Saxon – hated • wood • knight – attacked – defeated • Bonjour • gold • centuries

1 Scrambled words
Once upon a time • centuries • gold • knights • heir • hated • attacked • defeated

What do you remember?
Elephants – fave • Bonjour, mes petits. • Romeo, wherefore art thou Romeo • AD – Anno Domini • Salve • Valete • keep out • Hasta luego

2 Who says what?
1. attacked • defeated • Hasta luego
2. Salve • keeps out
3. Bonjour • knight • centuries • hated

What do you remember?
Protestant – Catholic • Elizabethan Age • poet • steam engine – invention – Industrial Revolution • workshop • power • steel factories • World War II – colonies – Empire – independent • European Union

3 History
The Roman Empire:
Hadrian's Wall, roads, inventions
The Elizabethan Age:
Shakespeare, Queen Elizabeth, poets, Protestant
The Industrial Revolution:
workshop, steam engine, inventions, steel, factories
The British Empire:
Queen Victoria, colonies, India

What do you remember?
wax • dresses • Was – able to • negative form – following • 'm not allowed to – have to – No way • action – stage • modern • Britons

4 Modal auxiliaries and their substitutes
1. wasn't able to • had to
2. will be allowed to
3. wasn't allowed to

5 How to visit a museum
1. Are there special prices for students?
2. Where can I buy souvenirs?
3. Can you tell me the way to the room about the British Empire, please?

What do you remember?
open day • suggestions • Making suggestions • prepare • suggested • ought to

6 Making suggestions
Do you have any suggestions about what to show him? • I want to show him the city centre. We could go there by bus. • How about a trip to the Museum of German History? • Why don't you check the prices on the Internet? • That's a good idea. You could also phone the museum.

7 Find the word
1. elephant 2. power 3. open day
4. dress 5. Bonjour!

What do you remember?
hot – Victorian • prison • empress • reign • throne • raw materials • fortress – towers • past perfect • free – farmers • slums – floor – clean • government

8 Lost vowels
1. The government made the suggestion that farmers should get more money.
2. The action in Shakespeare's plays happened on stage.
3. In the Victorian age Queen Victoria was on the throne and she was also empress of India.

What do you remember?
Get ready • is – about • pre-reading • gist – details • are – connected • close – connecting line

9 Reading activities
Pre-reading:
look at the title, look at the pictures, guess what the story could be about, guess who the characters could be
First reading:
read the story quickly, find out the most important ideas
Second reading:
read the story slowly, make a list of interesting words, look up important words, find headings for the different parts
A closer look:
compare the different characters

What do you remember?
servant – Lady – feed • lonely • sixth sense – strange visions • cleaning the fountain – odd • drowned • Such – girlfriend – whoever – wherever • metal flying • had no idea

10 Odd word out
1. Catholic 2. girlfriend 3. exciting 4. go

11 Bits and pieces
servant, lonely, prison, modern, empress, prepare, action, power, fountain, vision, detail, farmer

What do you remember?
lord • old-fashioned – jewellery • gasped – telegram • Actually – ghost • wondered – joking • reply

12 Opposites
1. boyfriend 2. to hate 3. lord 4. clean 5. gist
6. normal 7. to open 8. old-fashioned 9. to reply

13 Crossword puzzle
1. government 2. empire 3. slum 4. prison
5. fountain 6. servant

Solution: vision

What do you remember?
paragraph – ending • to continue • click – line • great-great-grandmother • curious – shining • nodded • middle name

14 Synonyms
1. replied 2. lonely 3. strange 4. the following
5. continue 6. drowned

15 Spot the mistakes
1. Ben**'s** great-great-**grand**mother nodded after she had listen**ed** to the details.
2. E-mails are **more modern** than telegra**ms** and they are also **faster**.

What do you remember?
Stress • stress

16 French words in English
famille – family • depart – departure • changer – change • grands-parents – grandparents • cousin – cousin • visiteur – visitor • théâtre – theatre • acteur – actor

17 Word search

G	F	C	A	D	I	F	F	E	R	E	N	T	B	R	E	M	P
E	E	D	I	A	L	O	G	U	E	Z	B	Y	D	F	M	X	R
C	A	D	F	G	H	U	T	V	H	Z	O	U	G	D	U	C	O
H	I	S	T	O	R	Y	X	G	A	C	T	I	O	N	S	R	B
R	V	T	I	U	R	C	B	Z	A	D	T	S	V	E	I	V	L
M	U	Y	Y	A	S	E	F	B	N	M	L	D	A	N	C	E	E
A	S	C	V	B	R	O	C	H	U	R	E	F	B	T	M	M	M

different, history, action, dance, brochure, bottle, music, problem, dialogue, city

18 Sentence stress
1. The **poet** William **Shakespeare** lived in the **Elizabethan** Age and wrote the **famous** play **Romeo** and **Juliet**.
2. In the **18th century** there was the **Industrial Revolution**, a time of many **inventions** like the **steam engine**.
3. The **British Empire** was the **age** when **Britain** had many **colonies** and **Queen Victoria** was on the **throne**.

19 Crossword puzzle
Across:
2. wax 4. free 5. age 8. stress 10. gold 11. slum
13. factory 14. detail 15. shine 16. negative
17. vision 18. invention 19. curious

Down:
1. fave 3. heir 6. gasp 7. poet 9. empire
9. modern 13. fortress

Revision Unit 1 + 2

1 Scrambled words: People

1. **umpire:**
   the person who controls a tennis match
2. **Catholic:**
   Many people who go to church are Catholic.
3. **poet:**
   a person whose job is to write poems
4. **American:**
   Someone who comes from the USA is American.
5. **knight:**
   someone who rides a horse and fights
6. **athlete:**
   a person who does / plays a sport
7. **empress:**
   a woman who's on the throne of a country
8. **heir:**
   the person who gets the money of someone who has died
9. **farmer:**
   This person makes and sells products like milk, meat or vegetables.
10. **servant:**
    This person works for other people and helps them.
11. **lady:**
    the wife of a lord
12. **scientist:**
    This person does research or works on inventions.

2 Word search

G	K	R	A	T	D	H	F	U	B	A	S	E	D	J	O	K	E	N
A	Q	M	A	R	A	T	H	O	N	O	N	O	A	R	N	B	B	F
S	A	G	R	E	E	I	N	G	G	E	G	D	W	R	C	F	B	C
P	C	L	W	D	V	M	O	F	X	J	O	D	E	F	E	A	T	U
A	T	D	S	G	V	Y	D	F	H	K	E	K	L	L	P	U	Y	R
T	U	S	C	W	F	S	S	S	S	P	A	S	V	A	I	D	G	I
A	A	O	V	O	E	A	T	P	O	W	E	R	D	P	D	N	M	O
X	L	O	L	N	E	V	G	Z	J	E	E	G	H	J	K	B	E	U
D	L	U	O	D	D	I	T	Y	D	A	O	A	F	C	B	T	B	S
F	Y	X	U	E	C	D	R	G	H	J	U	M	T	B	T	R	X	I
E	A	V	O	R	C	T	E	L	E	G	R	A	M	K	O	P	E	N

base, joke, marathon, agreeing, defeat, power, oddity, telegram, open, gasp, actually, wonder, flap, curious, feed, nod, odd, lines, once, sweat

Unit 3

What do you remember?

twins • behaves • tidies up • cleaning lady • drives me crazy • get on • each other • vegetarian • Brussels sprout • Eat up • frozen – microwave

1 Which words go together?

1. curly 2. lucky 3. a lie 4. crazy 5. fun
6. a suggestion 7. the way 8. his teeth 9. lost
10. the shopping

What do you remember?

marry • answerphone • split up • any more • bad luck • wise • selfish • I don't care • meet – or • DIY shop • hat • telephone

2 Sounds

1. Nina told a lie when she spoke to Frank at the party.
2. Eat up your burger, then we'll find out about the concert.
3. The kids get on well with their parents, but they don't agree about food or music.
4. I often look at TV programmes about interesting people.
5. George always makes his own pizzas and shares them with his old friend Andy.
6. Danny spends almost all his pocket money on expensive computer games or DVDs.

What do you remember?

in • grow • pip • crust • brushes her teeth • goes curly • tell a lie • 2L8 • UR • scenes

3 A puzzle

1. wise 2. teeth 3. frozen 4. meat 5. hat 6. luck
7. phone

Solution: stomach

What do you remember?

himself • old people's home • decided • extra • relax • enjoyed themselves • stand • turn – off

4 With or without '-self' / '-selves'?

themselves • myself • me • you • ourselves • it • himself • us • yourselves

What do you remember?

calls • gets dressed • helps herself • myself • itself • yourself

5 Dialogues

1. yourselves 2. himself 3. ourselves 4. themselves
5. myself

6 What did they do?

9, 4, 3, 7

What do you remember?

mind • difference • feels sorry for • earn • I see • you've got a point • meet halfway

7 Meeting halfway
That's sad! Why can't you come?
I see your problem. Is there an alternative?
That's a good idea. How about tomorrow?
OK, fine. I hope she says yes!

What do you remember?
probably • jealous • junk • wish • get rid of • turned – into • type • chat – especially • on chat • translate • advice

8 Odd word out
1. 'Wise' doesn't fit in because it isn't a negative word.
2. 'Purse' doesn't fit in because it isn't a person.
3. 'To brush' doesn't fit in because it doesn't have to do with what you want.
4. 'Junk' doesn't fit in because it's not something you give a person to reach a decision.
5. 'Comma' doesn't fit in because it's not something which you can put things into.

What do you remember?
didn't listen to • boyfriend • go out • secret • went crazy • agony aunt

9 The wrong word
1. gets angry 2. difference 3. sort out 4. go crazy 5. spends all his free time 6. I wish I could 7. going out with 8. split up

10 Tongue twisters
red lorry, yellow lorry
The sick sheikh's sixth sheep's sick.

What do you remember?
isn't in– take the call • Unfortunately – leave • tone • callers – voicemail • difficult • contact

11 A phone call
I'd like to talk to James. • Can I leave a message for him? • Please tell him that I'd like to meet him tomorrow. • I'd like to meet at 5 o'clock. • Yes, he can phone me at 0788 … • Thanks, bye.

What do you remember?
on his own • manage • grumpy • Shut up! – offered • home alone – doorbell • What's going on • guy • talk • First things first • one by one • make sure • get in the way • make a decision

12 Word pairs
1. nose • knows 2. threw • through 3. weak • week 4. meet • meat 5. seen • scene 6. hour • our

What do you remember?
put on • actresses • cast • costumes • witch • mask • props • lights • rehearse • rehearsal • audience • programme • curtain • applauds

13 Jumbled words: People and plays
2. actress 3. author 4. rehearsal 5. audience 6. director 7. actor 8. programme

14 Find the right pronoun
1. himself 2. you 3. myself 4. ourselves 5. it 6. me 7. themselves 8. it, themselves

15 Reflexive in German, not in English
1. remember 2. decide 3. hide 4. move 5. hurry 6. relax 7. queue

16 Stress the subject
1. herself 2. myself 3. yourselves 4. himself 5. ourselves 6. yourself 7. themselves

17 A crossword
Across:
4. difference 8. offer 9. doorbell 13. translate 16. curtain 18. managc 20. mind 21. rehearse 22. costume

Down:
1. difficult 2. jealous 3. actress 5. official 6. grumpy 7. secret 10. purse 11. earn 12. applaud 14. especially 15. guy 17. advice 19. audience

Unit 4

What do you remember?
region – heavy industry • coal mines – exist • facelift • landscape – less • contrast • recently – regional • On average • proud

1 Make new words or phrases
1. coal mine 2. facelift 3. high-tech industry 4. birthplace 5. landscape 6. old-fashioned

2 What's missing
1. recently 2. average 3. region 4. proud

What do you remember?
on the move • exchange • Welsh • move • birthplace • culture • cult • wing • male voice choir

3 A pairs puzzle
1. choir 2. Welsh 3. less 4. wings 5. regional 6. past

4 Missing words
1. of 2. for 3. on 4. on 5. at 6. about

What do you remember?
abstract • articles • definite article • indefinite • is into – bilingual • relatives • engineer – firm • would rather – the poor • awful – pair of • tea – friendship • taste

5 Abstract nouns
1. music 2. the home 3. love 4. home 5. the love 6. the music

What do you remember?
Dealing with problems – apologizing • deals with • Helping • apologize • I didn't mean to • Never mind • rude • Take your time

6 Helping and apologizing
7, 1 – 8, 6 – 3, 2 – 4, 5

7 Meeting new people
Lösungsvorschlag:
"Do you live near here?"
"Where do you go to school?"
"I'm at Franklin High School."
"Did you enjoy the concert?"
"Hello. I like your camera."

What do you remember?
Asian – up North • Punjabi • curry – tastes • smells – reply • Bhangra – exhibition • sound • audio – by • seemed

8 Verbs and adjectives – the odd word out
to sound – tasty – to taste – loud

9 'By' or 'until'?
1. by 2. until 3. by 4. until

What do you remember?
research • topic – leisure • factual texts – skim • concentrates – keywords • scan • Skimming – scanning • must-see • during • on land • conferences – motorway • dinner

10 Dialogues
1. scanning that text • I'm doing research
2. a must-see • during our journey
3. on the motorway • I must concentrate

What do you remember?
crowd • cheer • It's a pity • tried out – for fun • make fun of • accent – weird • Changing places • search engine • interactive • quite – get tired of • hang out • at least – waterfront

11 Find the word
1. English 2. interactive 3. waterfront 4. cheered 5. accent 6. hanging out

12 A word grid

N	I	J	L	H	P	A	C	Z	W	Y	E	M	P	X
E	X	H	I	B	I	T	I	O	N	J	O	O	C	Q
W	L	S	G	L	V	D	B	R	K	T	S	M	R	F
O	E	H	V	D	I	J	N	P	O	A	X	W	O	H
X	I	I	H	E	I	V	R	R	T	G	M	P	W	B
U	S	P	R	C	Q	T	W	N	A	B	I	S	D	Q
Z	U	A	L	D	L	A	N	D	S	C	A	P	E	J
I	R	K	I	C	Y	H	O	M	T	Z	Y	H	U	D
V	E	E	X	C	H	A	N	G	E	C	U	R	D	Q

exhibition, landscape, exchange, leisure, taste, crowd, weird, motorway

13 Singular or plural
1. three pairs of socks 2. a / one pair of jeans 3. a / one pair of goggles 4. two pairs of sunglasses 5. two swimsuits 6. three T-shirts

14 Adjectives from nouns
1. noisy 2. mountainous 3. colourful 4. adventurous 5. musical 6. healthy 7. powerful 8. cloudy

15 A crossword
Across:
3. apologize 4. birthplace 7. rather 9. fun 10. less 13. keyword 16. pity 19. crowd 21. leisure 22. taste 23. wings

Down:
1. relatives 2. move 5. recently 6. proud 8. awful 11. seem 12. bilingual 14. weird 15. dinner 17. accent 18. during 20. rude

Revision Unit 3+4

1 Odd word out
1. **difficult:** feelings
2. **leisure:** money
3. **engineer:** groups
4. **to seem:** language
5. **research:** theatre

2 What's the phrase?
1. That's a pity
2. Hm, you've got a point
3. 's/is driving me crazy
4. I didn't mean to be rude
5. I don't care
6. is making fun of me

3 How much do you remember?
Lösungsvorschlag:
culture:
cast, costume, cult, Welsh, facelift, male voice choir, bilingual, Asian, exhibition, Bhangra, audio, research, must-see, leisure, accent
at home:
to brush one's teeth, microwave, cleaning lady, answerphone, to turn off/on, to get dressed, old people's home, to relax, doorbell
getting on with people:
to tell a lie, to split, to get on, to behave, to drive so. crazy, to stand, to feel sorry for, to mind, to go out with, to apologize, rude

Unit 5

What do you remember?
celebrity • media – popular newspapers • quality newspapers • copy • studio • public • concert • created – awesome • copies

1 Odd one out
1. violence 2. concert 3. tips 4. Internet
5. product 6. teenager

2 Sounds: One sound makes a difference
1. made • mate 2. bag • back 3. foot • food

What do you remember?
programmes – entertainment • soap operas • advertise – soap – cleaning products – housewives • realistic • change • main – violence • nickname

3 Irregular verbs

Infinitive	Simple Past	Present Perfect
1. to break	broke	have/has broken
2. to show	showed	have/has shown
3. to write	wrote	have/has written
4. to choose	chose	have/has chosen
5. to teach	taught	have/has taught
6. to give	gave	have/has given
7. to take	took	have/has taken
8. to tell	told	have/has told
9. to bring	brought	have/has brought
10. to catch	caught	have/has caught
11. to grow	grew	have/has grown
12. to think	thought	have/has thought
13. to steal	stole	have/has stolen

What do you remember?
agent • script – discuss • photographed – file • assistant – film

4 False friends
a)
1. get 2. notes 3. skirt 4. kind 5. wants to
6. needn't / don't have to 7. lake

b)
1. (Land)karte 2. Bedeutung 3. Handlung
4. Reisebus 5. Turnschuhe • ausgeben

What do you remember?
sides • reread • cast • super • Don't get your hopes up too high • discovered • contract – by • sign

5 Wordsearch

N	N	E	W	S	P	A	P	E	R	O	T	C	A	R
E	D	V	C	O	M	M	E	R	C	I	A	L	N	P
W	I	Y	M	A	G	A	Z	I	N	E	H	C	W	L
S	C	R	I	P	T	A	D	V	E	R	T	I	S	E
L	M	O	B	I	L	E	M	M	A	R	G	O	R	P

newspaper, actor, commercial, magazine, script, advertise, mobile, programme, news, soap

6 Find the missing word
1. passive 2. to watch 3. cast 4. life 5. favourite
6. actresses

What do you remember?
couch potato • bookworm • maniac • discussing – pros and cons

7 What's in an ad?
hair • big • eyes • is wearing • white • black • is standing • are cheering • is smiling • has just shot • ad(vertisement) • picture • feeling • beautiful • winner

What do you remember?
advertising • ad(vertisement)s • are – worth – product – tube • get – attention – headline • soccer • look – smooth

8 Useful phrases: How to check each other's ad
If I were you, I would • I know what you mean. • It would be better if you • that's a good idea. • I think I'll do that. • I'll change that • Thanks.

What do you remember?
organised – LAN – raise money • attended • background – basic • allowed • noise • gave – opinion – rewritten • beginning • exchanged • argument • violent – police department

9 Verb friends

exchange	make	do
information	a mistake	homework
addresses	lunch	an exercise
ideas	a noise	the shopping

wear	attend
glasses	a party
trousers	a school
a helmet	a concert

What do you remember?
cereal • get him • convince • magic – pile – falls off – disappeared • ramp • cracked • cold – spinach • admit

10 Spot the mistake
1. ~~hairs~~ hair 2. ~~from~~ by 3. ~~a~~ some 4. ~~was~~ were
5. ~~drive~~ go 6. ~~show~~ shows 7. ~~meaning~~ opinion
8. ~~doesn't~~ don't

What do you remember?
walks past – above • roof – outline • gash • (has) cut • pipe • blood • emergency • ties – patient • distract • bandage – tight – ambulance • is rescued

11 Pronunciation

ʌ	enough	blood	trouble	country
au	allow	trousers	shout	ground
ei	great	raise	basic	plate

12 Word families
1. ad(vertisement) / advertising 2. blood 3. smell
4. feeling 5. invitation 6. flight

13 Be more polite
Lösungsvorschlag:
1. "Excuse me, you just pushed me." – "Oh, I'm very sorry. I should be more careful." – "That's OK. Never mind."
2. "Excuse me …" – "Can I help you?" – "Thanks, that's very kind of you!"
3. "Excuse me, could you tell me the time, please?" – "Of course. It's 10.15." – "Thank you!"

14 A mind map: Media

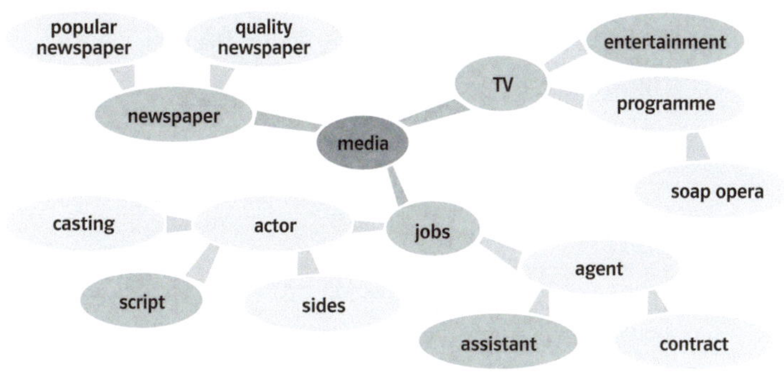

15 A crossword
Across:
1. housewives 5. spinach 7. signed 10. file
11. media 13. celeb 14. copy 15. kind 17. script
18. awesome 19. nickname 21. invite 23. noise
24. emergency 26. tie

Down:
2. song 3. entertainment 4. violence 6. commercial
7. soap 8. newspaper 9. bandage 12. beginning
16. smooth 18. active 20. tight 22. north 25. car

Unit 6

What do you remember?
travellers • evolution • Noodles – plant • journey – take • missionary • step – giant leap – mankind – moon • challenge • first language • per cent

1 Word puzzle
1. customs 2. arrival 3. take-off 4. departure 5. passport 6. baggage 7. passenger 8. ticket 9. airport

What do you remember?
report • introduce • mentioned – the day before • disappointing – two days earlier • welcome • had got – bored

2 Indirect speech with reporting verb in the past

Direct speech		Indirect speech
is	→	was
are going	→	were going
think	→	thought
writes	→	wrote
can	→	could
must	→	had to
may	→	might

Direct speech		Indirect speech
was/were	→	had been
saw	→	had seen
enjoyed	→	had enjoyed
had	→	had had
have/has done	→	had done
had visited	→	had visited
will know	→	would know

Direct speech		Indirect speech
here	→	here
this	→	this
come	→	go
bring	→	take
yesterday	→	the day before

Direct speech		Indirect speech
today	→	that day
tomorrow	→	the next day / the following day
last week	→	the week before
next year	→	the following year
two days ago	→	two days earlier

What do you remember?
advice • recommend • comedy • Who's in it • biography

3 Questions with prespositions
1. of 2. on 3. to 4. at/about 5. in 6. with

4 Talking about a film
1. It's a thriller. I can really recommend it. 4
2. Oh yes. It's one of the most exciting films I've ever seen. 8
3. If I tell you that, it might spoil it for you. 6
4. Have you seen Daniel Radcliffe's new film 'The Woman in Black'? 2
5. Well, you can at least tell me if it's exciting. 7
6. Cool, I like thrillers. What's it about? 5
7. No, not yet. What kind of film is it? 3
8. Can you recommend any good films? 1

What do you remember?
coach • dangerous chemicals • warned • trapped • service • Firefighters – paramedics • police officers – whether • asked • advised – area

5 An emergency call
help • I'm calling • burglar • noise • address • name • on my own • calm • officers

What do you remember?
right – annoying • fantastic – second language • extra – filler • And you

6 Jumbled sentences
1. Are you waiting for the train to Plymouth, too?
2. Yes, I am. I'm afraid it's running fifteen minutes late.
3. Oh dear, that is annoying. I have to be at the ferry port by 10.30.
4. Oh no! Are you going somewhere nice?
5. Yes, I'm going to Rennes.
6. Oh really? I've been there a few times. It's a beautiful place.
7. I'm sure you'll have a great time there.

What do you remember?
bet • railway • seats • princess – saved • complete • delay • make – on time • prairie • slows down • bellow – frightening – jumps out of her skin • track – buffalo

7 Scrambled words

M	E	N	T	I	O	N	S	D	P
A	C	R	E	X	P	L	A	I	N
S	W	A	L	B	M	R	Y	O	S
K	O	W	L	A	D	V	I	S	E

tell, warn, explain, say, ask, advise, mention

What do you remember?
continue • skin – on foot – danger • take the chance • whistle – side • screams • Sioux • shoot – guns – scream

8 Verbs and nouns with the same form
1. to drink • drinks 2. scream • screamed / was screaming 3. works • work 4. paint • paint

9 Make verbs from nouns

1. The roses smell beautiful.
2. Have you planned anything for this weekend?
3. After the game the sports star was interviewed by a reporter.

10 Same sounds – different words

1. weather • whether 2. they're • their • there 3. here • hear 4. where • wear 5. see • sea 6. write • right

11 Guess new words

a)
1. Aufruf, gehen Sie 2. Sicherheitshinweis, unbeaufsichtigt 3. Geräte, ausgeschaltet

b)
1. Erklärung, Entschuldigung 2. Schreck, kam/erschien 3. phantasievoll, unterhaltsam

12 Cryptogram

1	2	3	4	5	6	7	8	9	10	11
F	N	O	M	A	P	S	W	H	G	B

12	13	14	15	16	17	18	19	20	21	22
L	I	T	E	C	U	R	D	Y	J	V

1. buffalo 2. annoying 3. missionary 4. princess 5. paramedic 6. challenge 7. journey 8. firefighter 9. frightening 10. disappointing 11. traveller 12. burglar 13. scream 14. advice 15. recommend 16. whether 17. dangerous 18. railway 19. whistle 20. continue

Revision Unit 5 + 6

1 Word families

2. safety 3. violence 4. sun 5. difference 6. secret 7. friend / friendship 8. danger

2 Word groups

Jobs:
actress, nurse, agent, paramedic, police officer, firefighter
Travel:
baggage, travel agency, railway, passport, flight, motorway, coach
Media:
ad(vertisement), magazine, script, headline, newspaper report

3 Spot the mistake

1. ~~need~~ needed 2. ~~said~~ told 3. ~~all~~ everybody / everyone 4. ~~was my name~~ my name was 5. ~~to don't go~~ not to go 6. ~~is hurt~~ was hurt

4 Indirect speech

1. told / informed 2. said 3. advised / asked 4. warned

Bildquellenverzeichnis
U.1.1, U.4.1 Klett-Archiv, Stuttgart; **3.1** Ingram Publishing, Tattenhall Chester; **3.2** shutterstock (Kochergin), New York, NY; **3.3** shutterstock (Suzanne Tucker), New York, NY; **3.4** Fotolia LLC (RF/eblue), New York; **4.1** Getty Images RF (PhotoDisc), München; **7.1** Thinkstock (iStockphoto), München; **7.2** Thinkstock (Comstock), München; **7.3; 7.5** Avenue Images GmbH (image source), Hamburg; **7.4** Fotolia LLC (Michael Drager), New York; **10.1** Alamy Images (Brenda Prince), Abingdon, Oxon; **11.1** Getty Images, München; **22.1** iStockphoto (bobbieo), Calgary, Alberta; **22.2** iStockphoto (Sheryl Griffin), Calgary, Alberta; **22.3** Imago, Berlin; **22.4** Fotolia LLC (Monkey Business), New York; **22.5** Ingram Publishing, Tattenhall Chester; **30.1** Mauritius Images (Widmann), Mittenwald; **30.2** Thinkstock (Goodshoot), München; **30.3** Mauritius Images (Stock Image), Mittenwald; **30.4** Das Fotoarchiv RF (RF), Essen; **34.1** Fotosearch Stock Photography, Waukesha, WI; **40.1** iStockphoto (TheBiggles), Calgary, Alberta; **46.1** iStockphoto (George Argyropoulos), Calgary, Alberta; **54.1** Joker (David Ausserhofer), Bonn; **55.1** Klett-Archiv, Stuttgart; **57.1** iStockphoto (David Wilson), Calgary, Alberta; **64.1** Fotolia LLC (Franz Pfluegl), New York; **65.1** Klett-Archiv, Stuttgart; **66.1** Ingram Publishing, Tattenhall Chester

Sollte es in einem Einzelfall nicht gelungen sein, den korrekten Rechteinhaber ausfindig zu machen, so werden berechtigte Ansprüche selbstverständlich im Rahmen der üblichen Regelungen abgegolten.